"It Was Never My Fault. Still Triggered. Still Trying."

I0459184

Born to Bleed,

Built to Break,

Still Standing

A memoir of my life, "The pain they never saw, the silence that nearly killed me and what came after."

By

Faith Harris

Table of Contents

Prologue

"I was forged in silence, bruised by betrayal, and stitched back together with hope. My scars don't whisper weakness they speak of survival."

Some days, every breath feels like a betrayal. Like my own lungs are working against me, dragging me deeper into a battle I never chose.

Waking up means stepping into a war zone inside my mind, where dark voices whisper sharp lies: "You're better off gone. You don't deserve to exist."

Suicidality isn't a moment of weakness; it's a shadow that stalks me relentlessly.

Sometimes it's a faint, cold murmur beneath the noise.

Other times it crashes over me like a tidal wave, threatening to drown everything I am.

And still, I cling to the fight! I refuse to surrender; not today, not ever.

People say I'm strong, a survivor.

But they don't see the crushing weight I carry every second.

They don't see the endless war beneath my smile.

The exhaustion that seeps into my bones from years of being invisible, broken, and unloved.

They don't see the small, trembling girl inside, aching with the pain of a thousand wounds no one ever kissed better.

They don't see the little girl who never felt safe in the place she called home.

Who craved her mother's love only to be met with coldness and cruelty.

A mother who saw me as a burden,

whose arms were open for her other children but left me out in the cold,

blaming me for wanting, for needing, for existing.

Punishing me for every tear, every small hope, every breath I dared take.

They don't see the father who blurred the line between love and betrayal.

Who wrapped me in warmth one day and tore me apart in silence the next.

Who taught me that love could hurt, that trust was a trap,

that safety was just a lie whispered in the dark.

They don't see the layers beneath it all.

The grinding poverty that shrank my world and stole my innocence,

the bruises I hid beneath long sleeves and forced smiles,

the violence I learnt to mistake for love because it was the only language I understood.

They don't see the cycle of adult relationships echoing the hurt I was born into, where I chased pain just to feel something real, anything at all.

They don't see the legal systems that silenced me, the hollow echoes of my screams lost in empty rooms.

And they don't see the moment I tried to build a better life. When I opened my heart and home to a child I fostered. A child whose violence turned our world into a war zone. A child who nearly destroyed me and the fragile family I fought to hold together.

Yet the system, cold and unyielding, turned on me. Child protection didn't come with help or hope, only judgment. They painted me as the villain, the "bad parent."

And for so long, I believed them. Because they were the professionals, and I was barely surviving.

But deep in my bones, I know now they were wrong!

Was it the trauma passed down through generations, buried and ignored?

The suffocating silence swallowing the truth of abuse?

The partner who shattered the fragile life I'd built?

The diagnoses that came too late, or never came at all?

The ADHD and trauma carved into my very soul, desperate to be seen, to be heard, but dismissed until I stopped trying to speak?

I have lived 40+ years in survival mode.

Learnt many skills and talents to mask my pain, to fake strength,

to protect others while bleeding in silence.

And yet... somehow... here I am.

Life spun me wild; it broke me open, and still, I found purpose in the wreckage.

Now, I volunteer in suicide prevention, trying to build lifelines where I once had none.

I fight for change because no one should ever feel too broken to be saved.

I never thought I would live long enough to dream.

To hope, to want more, or be able to see change.

But through the darkness, fragile rays of sunlight pierce the gloom, slow and painful, yet fiercely beautiful.

I am still triggered... still fighting... not healed... not whole.

But no longer invisible... stumbling... determined not to fall.

This is not a story wrapped in neat healing or easy answers.

This is the story of a girl born into violence, shaped by trauma, and still standing, breath by breath, becoming something no one thought possible.

LIVING ... HEALING ... SOME PLACE NEW ...

And in this survival, I carry something unexpected, a flicker of hope, small and fragile like a candle in the darkest night.

It doesn't erase the pain; it doesn't pretend the scars aren't there.

But it whispers that maybe, just maybe, there is a future worth fighting for there.

A life where the weight lifts, if only for a moment. Where dreams feel a little closer,

and the next breath might just be a little easier.

Hope isn't a promise; it's the decision I keep making, every single day, to stay.

Because even in the deepest, darkest nights, there is always the possibility of dawn.

* All names and places have been changed for privacy and confidentiality.

** Trigger warning: this book contains content relating to domestic violence, childhood abuse, sexual abuse, eating disorders, bullying, self-harm, suicide, drugs, and alcohol. If you are feeling impacted, please refer to the end of the book for services to assist you.

Chapter 1: Bloodlines and Bruises

Poem – Whispered Truth

I was a child with open hands, just wanting to be held, someone to understand, not broken.

I reached for love, but found fists, found silence, found shame dressed as motherhood.

I learnt to whisper apologies for bruises I didn't cause, to comfort the woman who hurt me, to soothe her tears after her rage.

His voice was kind until it wasn't. His hands, safe until they weren't. And every time I flinched, every time I froze, they called it my fault.

I begged to be seen. I called for help. But they turned their backs and let the house swallow my screams.

So, I became small. Timid. A shadow.

Her voice became my mirror. Her insults my reflection. Her blame my gospel.

And every time I thought maybe I was good, that voice dragged me back, snarled, "Don't be so full of yourself."

This is not just a story. This is my resurrection. From beneath the rubble of lies, this is my voice, taking back its name.

"Before I even knew what love was, I learnt what it wasn't, in the silence, the blame, the touch that stole my name, and the eyes that looked away."

There are two people who gave me life, but also shaped the cage I was raised in.

We lived in a cold, weathered yellow house made of plastic weatherboard. It sat perched halfway up a steep hill, as if it had been dropped there and forgotten. The tin roof leaked when it rained, and the sound of water dripping into buckets became a lullaby I never asked for.

The carpet inside was frayed, thinned from years of wear, and had shrunk away from the edges of the rooms like it, too, wanted to escape. The kitchen looked part new, part wreck. That was because, one afternoon, my mum left lunch on the stove for my dad and wandered next door. The result was a fire. Flames licked up the walls and burnt away the old kitchen. What stood in its place never quite matched the rest of the house. Nothing ever really fit right.

The backyard was large, split into levels by a rough old retaining wall. My dad had carved out a massive vegetable garden. A patch of earth that fed us more than any supermarket ever did.

We had animals: two dogs, two cats, a rabbit, and a cage of ferrets that stank no matter how often it was cleaned. From a distance, it might've looked like a place full of life, but for me, it was a house haunted by everything unspoken.

To the outside world, my mother was warm and radiant, the kind of woman who'd go out of her way to help someone in need. She called my friends behind my back, pretending to care, asking questions like a concerned parent. She smiled in public, laughed loudly, and collected sympathy like it was currency. But that version of her only existed where people could see.

Behind the curtains, she was venom and cruelty wrapped in flesh. I wasn't her daughter; I was her target. She made sure I knew I was in the way. Worthless. Useless. Always wrong.

She told me I ruined her life, that I was a burden, that I should shut up and disappear. She'd scream at me to leave, then scream again when I did. Push me away, then punish me for the distance. Her rules were written in disappearing ink, and no matter what I did, I was already guilty.

Her voice didn't just echo in the house. It became the voice inside my head. Her accusations and cruelty became the truths I lived by. I was ugly. Disgusting. A mistake. A problem. A girl no one would ever love.

I began to repeat it to myself without her even needing to say it. "I ruin everything." "I'm stupid." "I should've never been born." "I don't deserve kindness." "Everything is my fault."

Every slap, every hair pull, every belt, every kick, every scream, every moment of silence when I needed comfort. It all became a mirror that told me who I was: nothing. I wasn't worth defending. Not by her. Not by him. Not by the neighbours who looked away. Not by the kids' helpline that hung up.

She never told me she loved me. Never hugged me. Instead, she silenced me with her bitterness and punished me with her rage. But when she wanted comfort, I was expected to become the mother.

Wiping her tears during her breakdowns, holding her through her tantrums, soothing her storm. I remember her clinging to me as she cried, mascara smudged, breath sour, blaming me between sobs. "Look what you made me do," she'd wail, gripping my arms too tightly, leaving bruises I had to explain away. If I wiped her tears the wrong way, she'd scream at me. If I flinched, she'd hit me again. I became her tissue, her therapist, her prisoner.

Once, I held the screen door open for her because her hands were full. She couldn't get the key into the lock fast enough and screamed at me. Then she shoved me. I flew backward, crashing through a rose bush and landing hard on the concrete path.

Thorns tore through my skin, and my wrist snapped under the weight of the fall, and I bit through my lip. I lay there winded, the taste of blood in my mouth, dirt in my wounds. She stood over me, her face twisted with annoyance, not concern. "Get up. You're fine. Stop being dramatic." No hugs. No apologies. Just orders.

Days later, when my wrist still wouldn't move without screaming pain, she finally took me to a doctor, but only after rehearsing a lie. I was to say a dog jumped up on me. I nodded, already knowing better than to tell the truth.

She was always the victim. Always sick. A new illness every week, a new story to tell. But when I truly needed a doctor (when I was starving myself, holding my breath in hopes I'd die, or when I limped from bruises and breaks), she denied me care. Real pain wasn't allowed. Only hers.

She made me shower with her. Baths weren't allowed. She'd plug the drain so the water pooled at our feet, then press a soaked face washer over my mouth and nose. When I gasped, she rubbed soap into my eyes until I couldn't see. If I struggled, she'd shove me under the water, holding me down, her hand heavy on the back of my head. I learnt not to scream; it only made it worse.

My father was different. At first.

He was gentle. Loving. The safe one. When Mum's violence became too much, he'd take me for a drive until I fell asleep in the car, letting the quiet hum of the road lull me into peace.

He came from a big, close family. He loved fishing and hunting and growing things in the garden. He listened. He never judged. He tried to keep the peace.

But over time, she wore him down too. She made him feel guilty for leaving the house without her. Slowly, he stopped doing the things he loved.

He buried himself in work, sleeping at his job in a toxic tire retreading factory just to make ends meet. He took on extra loads for cash. He was trying to provide, but he was disappearing.

Then he changed.

I found my money box, the one I'd saved so carefully, empty, in the back of his car. He told me I must've lost it. I wanted to believe him. But I knew.

And then came the dog.

I wanted her to sleep in my bed. For comfort. For love. For safety. I begged. I pleaded. But Mum said no and raged. She screamed that I was ungrateful, that I didn't deserve anything. Then she turned to Dad. Her voice lowered, sharpened. "Take care of it." I didn't understand. Not fully. Until he did.

I remember the sound first. The metallic click of the rifle being cocked. Then the whimper. My dog, Spot, tail tucked, ears back, eyes wide, sensed something was wrong. She looked at me, as if I could stop it. I ran down the hill toward her, where she was tied up, screaming, "Don't!"

He aimed.

The gunshot cracked through the air like lightning. I watched her body drop. Her yelp ripped through me like a knife. I fell to my knees, screaming, unable to move. She twitched. Once. Twice. Then nothing. I felt the silence more than the sound. Deafening. My chest heaved. My mouth opened, but no sound came out anymore.

He walked away.

And I knew this was how love was betrayed, in my house.

But the worst betrayal didn't scream or shout. It whispered. It pretended. It came quietly with coffee breath, cigarette smoke, and rough hands. He did things to me no father should do to a daughter.

His hands, the same ones that used to pick tomatoes, fix cars, lift me into his lap, became foreign, violent, invasive. He touched me in silence. Hurt me in silence. And then, like nothing had happened, he'd bring me a block of chocolate. A packet of chips. A smile.

I didn't have the words. But I had the knowing. That something inside me broke every time. That I wasn't safe, not even with the person I once trusted most.

Sometimes I wondered if the treats were hush money. Chocolate and chips in exchange for secrets I didn't have the language to tell.

At night, I curled up on the top bunk, every doll in my bed tucked in as a barricade. I slept in a tight ball against the wall, praying I'd be invisible. The kitchen reeked of cigarette smoke. The radio was always on, the television humming from

11

my mother's bedroom, even at 2 a.m. The air was stale. The fear was thick. If I needed the toilet, I dragged my sister with me. She wasn't scared. She was loved.

I'll tell you about her and my other sibling in the next chapter.

I tried to ask for help. I called Kids Helpline, whispering my pain, trying to explain through trembling sobs. But they said maybe I misunderstood. Maybe it wasn't that bad. Maybe I should talk to someone at school. No one came. No one followed up. No one saved me.

Our neighbours must have heard the yelling. They saw the bruises. They saw how I flinched, how I limped, how I lied. They saw the fear on my face. But they said nothing. Did nothing. I guess it was easier that way.

My dad stole clothes left beside charity bins. My mum paraded our home like it was normal while neighbours turned a blind eye. I was ashamed of our poverty, of the way we lived, of the lies I was told to tell. I tried to make sense of it. Tried to please her. Begged her to tell me what she needed. But she never cared what I needed.

I believed it must be normal. That all families were like this. That maybe I was the problem. Dumb. Useless. Stupid. Disgusting. Broken. Rotten. Pathetic. Filthy. Attention-seeking. Unlovable.

But the truth is I was a child. A child who should have been protected.

And no one did.

So I silenced myself to survive. But inside, my mind was a war zone. Fighting for understanding. Begging for someone to see. Hoping that somehow, someday, my voice would matter.

This is that voice. This is the truth they tried to bury. This is where it begins.

Chapter 2: The Chosen Ones

Poem: The Price of the Golden Glow

They wore crowns of light, polished and praised,

While I knelt in corners, silenced and dazed.

They were the chosen, the adored, the seen,

While I scrubbed the floor of a kingdom unclean.

Their laughter was echoed, their mess ignored,

My cries were punishments, my truth abhorred.

They broke the rules with grins and cheers,

I bore the beatings, the blame, the tears.

A gumboot's arc, a shattered glass,

The truth was buried, just like the past.

A shed, a scream, a lock turned tight,

And no one asked where I was that night.

They called me liar, filthy, wrong,

And so I learnt to make pain my song.

Better to ache than feel so alone,

Better to hurt than turn to stone.

I learnt the art of staying small,

Of disappearing inside each wall.

Not seen, not heard, not safe, not whole,

Just survival stitched into my soul.

"In a house built on fear, the golden children never get dirty even when their hands are full of dust."

David was the first. The golden boy. Born when Mum was just nineteen and newly married, he was her prize, her redemption, her savior in a world she hadn't yet figured out. He arrived before the bruises became daily, before the screaming became routine, and so he was untouched by it, or maybe he was protected from it. Either way, it was clear: David could do no wrong.

He had the best room in the house. Painted exactly how he wanted, filled with shelves of things he had chosen. Everything was new: nothing secondhand, nothing handed down. He was allowed to decorate it with posters and toys, and not once was he told it was too messy or not good enough. It was his space. His safe haven. I never had one of those.

David was Dad's shadow, walking beside him like he was already a man. And to Mum, he was her favorite, her firstborn and a boy. The one who smiled just right and who never got blamed. He never had to do chores. No one yelled at him for leaving a plate out or for staying up too late. Mum asked about his day. She laughed at his jokes. She cared.

To everyone else, David was the popular one, the one with all the mates in the street. But behind closed doors, he was a tormentor. My tormentor.

He'd burst into my room uninvited, throw things, call me names, try to provoke a reaction. I learnt that silence was the safest response. That if I ignored him, maybe he'd get bored and walk away. But he learnt that too, that I wouldn't fight back, that I wouldn't scream. So, he kept pushing, looking for a fight.

One day, I remember, he was throwing gumboots at my head when Mum wasn't home. I snapped. I picked one up and threw it back. He dodged, and it smashed straight into Mum's glass cabinet.

I panicked. I ran. I lied. I said he did it. Not because I wanted to hurt him, but because I knew what would happen if I told the truth. I was scared. I was always scared.

Mum didn't get angry. Well, not right then. She just laughed with her friend when I told the story, didn't even pause her cuppa. But when we got home and she asked David what happened, he, for once, told part of the truth. It was, in fact, me who had thrown the boot, and that was enough.

My story didn't matter. The reasons didn't matter. I was the menace, the troublemaker, the one who needed to be punished. And punished I was, hard, fast, and without any space to explain.

Then there was the time he locked me in the dog shed. It was dark, no windows, just wood and tin pressed in like a tomb. I'd gone in to clean it.

He followed, and while I was inside, he slammed the door shut and locked it. I screamed. I kicked. I begged. He laughed. I bashed at the door until my hands split, until my throat ached. No one came. No one even noticed I was gone. When I was finally let out, it was night and I was sent straight to bed, hungry. No dinner. Nothing.

But the worst memory, the one that lives inside my bones, was the day I was sent next door with David and the neighbor's son. I was told we were going to cook something. What happened instead was unthinkable. They made me lie down. They took off my clothes. My brother, the neighbor, and his cousin.

I don't remember everything; I just remember the laughter, the fear, the silence that took over my body like a fog. I remember the neighbor's mum walking in and screaming at me! Not them. Calling me filthy, disgusting, telling me to get out. Like I had asked for it. Like I had wanted it. It was all my fault!

I believed her. I believed all of them. Because I was a kid. And they were adults. And my brother was the golden one.

David went on weekend trips with Dad—fishing, hunting, shooting. He was allowed to use a gun. He went with Dad to work during the holidays, though I never knew exactly what they did. I didn't want to know. Not after the things I knew about both of them and what they did to me. The way they talked about girls, the way they looked at them, and what they did to me: I would never trust them to be completely clean.

Not long before he left home, David was caught shoplifting. Mum and Dad whispered about it behind closed doors. But I found the truth: a tape of the police interview. He had gone in alone, stolen jelly cups and lollies, couldn't be bothered lining up. But the story Mum told? His mates made him do it. Of course they did.

Later he was in a motorbike accident. They found weed in his system. But the truth didn't matter. He was just a poor boy who made mistakes. Never mind the growing, the using, or the dealing.

Then there was my sister Lisa.

She was 14 months younger than me. Fiery. Loud. Demanding. She made herself heard. So she, too, always got what she wanted.

She had asthma as a child and knew how to use it. She was cuddled, adored, cared for. She got the late-night movie marathons, the one-on-one time with Mum. I watched from a distance.

She screamed back when David tormented her, so he backed off. With me, he got silence. With her, a fight.

But the house echoed with her noise: slamming doors, shrieking laughter, tantrums. And somehow, it was always my fault.

I shared a room with her. She was messy. Clothes everywhere, wrappers under the bed, chaos in every corner. But I was the one who got yelled at to clean it.

At night, if she was bored, she would stir things up just to see me get hurt. She'd bang on the walls, whisper loudly, stomp around.

Mum would come storming in. She never asked. Never listened. Just grabbed. Whatever she could reach, my leg, arm, hair, and yanked me from the top bunk to the floor. Then my pants down, then the smacks, broom, wooden spoon, belt. I learnt not to cry. Crying made it worse.

Instead, I started to like the pain. Because it gave me something to feel. Something that wasn't shame. Something that wasn't blame. My sister giggled under her blankets, never lifting a finger to help.

She stole, too. Once, she took Dad's entire paycheck and hid it under her pillow. Nothing happened. Not a word. If that had been me, I'd have been bruised, bloodied, barely breathing. But she was special. The fire-watching, TV-hogging, sleepover-hosting, never-bathing favorite.

She got to be; I just had to cope.

Looking back now, the patterns are obvious. David and Lisa were the golden children. The light of the house, the ones who could do no wrong.

I was the scapegoat, the invisible one. The one they pointed at when anything broke, when anything went missing, when anything felt wrong.

I became the quiet one, the small one, the problem. I wasn't allowed needs; I wasn't allowed truth. I was forced to carry their mess and wear it like it was mine.

So, as I entered kinder and primary school, I took that deep belief that I was the cause of everything bad: I was just worthless and needed to stay silent.

Reflection: - Childhood Abuse and Neglect Through Lived Experience

When people think of childhood abuse, they often picture obvious violence, bruises, broken bones, screaming fights. The truth is that abuse and neglect often live in the ordinary, hidden behind curtains, smiles, and excuses. To the outside world, it can look like a normal family. To the child inside it, it feels like a war zone where love is conditional, safety doesn't exist, and silence is the only protection.

I know this because I lived it. My childhood wasn't defined by one kind of abuse; it was all of them. Each left its mark; each whispered its own lie about who I was and what I deserved.

Together, they shaped my core beliefs in ways that followed me into adulthood.

The Wounds

- **Physical abuse** taught me I deserved pain.
- **Emotional abuse** taught me I was worthless.
- **Psychological abuse** taught me I wasn't real.
- **Sexual abuse** taught me my body wasn't mine.
- **Neglect** taught me my needs didn't matter.

The lasting wound wasn't just the bruises or hunger but the belief I carried: I am broken, unlovable, and to blame.

I learnt to freeze, be still, silent, invisible, because stillness felt safer than resistance. I learnt to fawn, pleasing, appeasing, smoothing over anger, because maybe, if I was useful enough, I could avoid harm. These were not weaknesses; they were survival. Brilliant, instinctive adaptations to impossible circumstances.

But survival has a cost. Freeze and fawn responses didn't disappear when childhood ended. They came with me into adulthood, into relationships, workplaces, friendships. I apologized too much. I avoided conflict at any cost. I stayed small, even when it hurt.

The Truth About Healing

Abuse and neglect don't just break bones; they fracture the blueprint for love, trust, and identity. But here's what I've learnt on the other side: those blueprints can be rewritten.

With therapy, support, and courage, I discovered that healing isn't about pretending the past didn't happen; it's about facing the truths I once had to suppress to survive.

- You can rewrite your core beliefs.

- You can allow feelings to return, and finally release the guilt, shame, and blame that were never yours to carry.
- You can separate what happened from who you are: yes, this happened to me, but it is not me.
- You can grow from your pain and even learn from it, instead of being defined by it.
- You can rebuild trust, regain self-worth, and step into a life that feels like your own.

Recovery is not a straight line; it's messy, exhausting, and full of setbacks, but it is possible. I know this because I am living proof. The child who once believed she was invisible now speaks her truth. The adult who carried silence like armor now uses her voice to break it.

What Survivors Need Most

When people ask, "Why didn't you tell someone?" this is the answer: I did. I called a helpline. I tried to show teachers. Neighbors saw. But silence and disbelief confirmed the lies I already believed. If no one defends you, you assume you don't deserve defending.

This is why understanding abuse matters. It isn't just about bruises or headlines. It's about the invisible ways children are silenced, the lifelong wounds that form when no one steps in, and the false truths that become a child's identity.

The lies they taught me are not mine to own. They belonged to the people who failed me. I was never worthless, never dirty, never to blame. I was a child who deserved safety, protection, and love.

If you want to know how to help, whether it's a child living through it right now or an adult still carrying the weight, here's what makes the difference:

For a Child Living in Abuse or Neglect

☑ **Do:**

- **Believe them**. If a child discloses something, even if it seems small, take it seriously. Belief can be the first seed of hope.

- **Protect them**. Take action. Report. Follow through. Your courage could change the entire course of their life.

- **Notice the signs.** Bruises, sudden changes in behaviour, hunger, withdrawal, over-compliance; these are not "phases." They are silent cries for help.

- **Offer consistency**. Show up reliably. For a child who only knows chaos, one safe adult can be life-changing.

- **Validate their feelings**. Say: "This is not your fault. You don't deserve this. You are not bad." Words like this can undo years of lies.

- **Create safe spaces**. Even small moments of play, laughter, or kindness remind a child that love without harm exists.

✗ **Don't:**

- Don't dismiss with "Maybe you misunderstood" or "It's not that bad." This deepens their silence.

- Don't blame them. Abuse is never a child's fault.

- Don't ignore the signs. Waiting for someone else to act often means no one will.

- Don't make promises you can't keep, like "I won't tell." Instead, say: "I need to get help to keep you safe."

- Don't assume silence means safety. Many children freeze or fawn. Compliance often hides fear.

Message of hope: Even if you can't erase what's happened, you can be the person who shows a child that love can be safe and unconditional. Sometimes one safe adult is enough to plant the belief: I matter. I am worth protecting.

For an Adult Survivor of Childhood Abuse or Neglect

☑ **Do:**

- **Believe them.** When someone shares their childhood truth, honour it. Their courage to speak is part of their healing.

- **Listen without judgment.** Let them tell their story in fragments or in full. Trust that how it comes is how trauma memory works.

- **Acknowledge the harm.** Simple words like "What happened to you was wrong. You didn't deserve that. I'm sorry no one protected you" can bring deep relief.

- **Respect their boundaries.** Survivors often need control over touch, space, or trust. Honor that without question.

- **Encourage healing.** Therapy, peer groups, creativity, movement: healing is not one-size-fits-all. Support them in whatever feels right.

- **Be patient.** Trust and self-worth take time to rebuild. Showing up consistently matters more than quick fixes.

✕ **Don't:**

- Don't minimize with "That was a long time ago" or "At least it made you strong." Trauma does not fade with years.

- Don't demand proof. Memories can be fragmented and still be true.

- Don't shame coping strategies. Addiction, withdrawal, perfectionism; these are survival, not weakness.

- Don't push for details. Survivors will share when they feel safe enough.

- Don't compare pain. Healing is not a competition.

- Don't pressure them to "get over it." Healing is lifelong, and survivors need compassion more than timelines.

Message of hope: Supporting an adult survivor is about more than listening; it's about walking alongside them as they reclaim what was stolen. Healing is not about forgetting the past but finding the freedom to live fully beyond it.

The Core Message

No child should ever be left unseen, unheard, or unprotected. And no adult survivor should ever be left to carry the weight of what was done to them alone.

Abuse thrives in silence, but healing grows in connection. Every act of listening, every moment of protection, every word of validation helps rewrite the survivor's story:

From "I am broken" to "I am whole."

From "I am unlovable" to "I am worthy."

From "This is my shame" to "This was never mine to carry."

Chapter 3: When Play Wasn't Safe

Poem: While They Played

While they played,

I watched

small hands clenched,

legs tucked in tight,

pretending I liked being alone.

Their laughter rose

like wind through trees,

while I sat

still,

stone-hearted,

learning not to feel.

My sister ran,

kicked, screamed,

pushed the danger back.

But I stayed.

I froze.

And the guilt of that silence

still echoes in me.

I wanted to scream.

I wanted to run.

I wanted to be

one of the children

who didn't carry a secret

inside their skin.

But I was the quiet one,

too scared to move,

too broken to speak,

wondering why my fear

didn't look like hers.

"The world told me childhood was meant for joy, but mine came with rules, secrets, and scars."

I used to believe what the books said, that childhood was soft, safe. That it came with sunshine and lullabies and arms that reached for you when you cried. But mine came wrapped in silence. In rules I didn't understand and secrets that made my stomachache.

I was a child made of shrinking. I lived small, breath shallow, voice quiet, eyes always scanning for danger. Play wasn't safe, joy wasn't mine.

Mum told me my grandmother (her mother) adored me. That as her first granddaughter, I was not only special, but I was also wanted and loved. But Mum's words bent truth like soft metal. I never knew which parts were real and which were meant to control me.

When I try to remember Grandma, all I can see is the sunroom. It smelt like varnish and old fruit bowls, and the floorboards creaked like they were whispering. Outside in the back garden, there was a tall walnut tree, loaded branches drooped heavy with brown shells.

I would pick them and bring them into the sunroom where I'd stomp on them, one by one, pretending I was strong enough to break something. It gave me a tiny moment of power in a world that stole all the rest. Sunlight poured in through the windows, golden and warm, but it never reached my skin that was always covered by clothes stained and torn.

I felt cold in that house, like I didn't belong. It was like the light passed through me, not into me. Just as the gazes and looks from those around me did. Invisible, empty, unseen, unheard, just me in a bubble, my own little world.

Mum said Grandma had me often when I was little. That I was hers, in a way Mum could never fully claim. I wanted to believe that and fantasized about what that may look like. But when I reached for the feeling of love, there was only distance, like looking at a memory underwater.

I barely remember Mum's father. People said he was an alcoholic, but to me he was a shadow always on the edge of the picture. I only remember one visit.

He arrived at our house holding a small tin box. Inside were Grandma's ashes. He had carried her with him for years, tucked inside a handbag, unable to let her go. He handed her to Mum with grief in his eyes. I didn't understand then, but I felt it, his pain. It clung to him like a security blanket, like he and Grandma were complete again. After that, I never really saw him again. He drifted out of my life like fog lifting in the morning.

Dad's parents lived nearby, but their house was a place we rarely visited. Mum always had a reason not to go. Maybe it was jealousy, maybe it was power. Maybe she just wanted to keep Dad tethered only to her. I didn't question it. I simply knew we weren't welcome in that world. Or maybe we were, and Mum just didn't want us to be.

But the person I remember most, the one whose memory I wish I could erase, was my other Grandpa, my father's father.

In the driveway as you led up to their house was a shed. Not a place of tools and toys like on TV. This shed smelt like wet timber, rust, sweat, and old beer. The rubber flap on the door slapped gently in the wind like a taunt. The light inside was always wrong, too dim, too yellow, casting long shadows that swallowed everything good.

Every time we visited, my chest clenched before we even parked. The others would go into the house for tea, biscuits, conversations, and I would walk empty and numb toward the shed. My feet moved like they didn't belong to me. Like they were being pulled by something I couldn't fight.

The air inside was thick; it clung to my skin like something rotten. My heart beat so loudly I thought it might burst. He smelt, sweat and something sour that made me feel sick. He didn't speak. He never needed to.

He just grabbed.

His hands were hard and fast. He pulled me close. Made me touch, made me gag. I froze. Every time. My mind folded in on itself, turning off the parts that felt, the parts that screamed. I was too small to fight, too scared to run. I became stillness. Stillness kept me safe, or as safe as I could be while dying on the inside.

When it was over, he'd walk out like nothing had happened. I would follow him into the kitchen. Tea made warm in my own special mug, home-baked biscuits that I enjoyed so much. Smiles and laughter, Grandma's cheerful voice, but no one asked where I'd been or why I was late. No one noticed the weight I dragged behind me like an anchor.

I never told, not because I didn't want to. But because silence was the only thing I'd ever learnt how to do. Silence was safer; who would believe me, that creaky, soft, broken voice that spoke from within me. Speaking was danger, met with dismissal and punishment. This I learnt hurt a lot less.

Kindergarten was supposed to be a safe place. Bright colors, fun, mess, music, soft toys, play, and warm snacks. But I didn't talk. I sat alone, knees tucked to my chest, eyes watching the world from the shadows. Other children played in noisy flocks, laughter like birdsong. I stayed quiet, small, invisible, and broken.

I was smart. I could draw, build, solve puzzles faster than the others. But I didn't speak, not because I couldn't, but because I didn't know how to exist in a world where inclusion and loud were okay; I didn't know how to be a kid in any way.

Asking for the toilet felt too risky, so sometimes I didn't. I just stayed still until it was too late; wetting myself felt less scary than being seen. The shame and embarrassment burnt deep. I pretended nothing happened and waited for the clock to tell me I could go home.

They said I wasn't ready to attend school, that I needed to repeat another year of kindergarten before trialing school. No one asked why, no one wondered what might've been keeping me so quiet. They just wanted to see me be like the others.

Then I met Amanda.

Amanda had horses, cows, and open fields and a house that smelt like cinnamon and sunshine. At her place, I could run. I could laugh. I could feel, just for a moment, like maybe I belonged.

But then one day that safe place turned.

Amanda began touching me in ways that made something inside me curl up. At first, I thought maybe this was just what friends did. I didn't want to lose her; I didn't want to lose the safety of her house. I didn't know how to say no. My body froze, just like it always did. Silent, obedient, confused, and breaking within.

Years later, she told me someone at church had hurt her, too. I couldn't tell her my truth. Now I held her secret locked up with mine too. We were both children walking through fire, reaching for each other in the dark. But our silence didn't heal anything; it just built walls around us.

Primary school was chaos; the halls were loud and the classrooms too bright. The noise was a constant drumbeat in my head, confusion about which conversation to listen to, so I got lost instead. I kept my head down, did every task with perfection, never asked questions, rarely made mistakes. My worth lived in neat handwriting and correct answers, in being invisible and obedient.

The classroom was peace. It was heaven. No one touched me there. No one yelled. I sat at the back, quiet, watching the window while pretending to be okay.

But recess was a war zone.

The other kids ran wild, screaming, laughing, playing games I didn't understand. I couldn't catch a ball. I couldn't join in. I perched on a brick pillar and cried silently, the sting of not-belonging sharper than the wind.

I didn't know how to be a child, not really, and it frustrated me and filled me with envy. My stories were full of shadows. My body didn't know what joy felt like. I watched the others, aching to be like them—normal, light, and free—but I didn't have the map.

At home, when Mum got tired of me, she sent me to the park. She didn't want to watch me, didn't want to hear or speak to me. The park became another battlefield. Older boys waited there, cruel boys. They shoved me, spit at me, chased and pinned me. Called me names, hit and kicked until I stopped trying to stand up.

I told Mum.

"You must have done something to make them angry," she said. "Don't be a freak."

Her words were knives. Sharper than fists.

Sometimes the soft drink truck driver would let me ride on the back tray of the truck. For a few sweet minutes, wind filled my lungs, the sky stretched wide, and I felt almost free. Like I was flying. But then the rules changed. I wasn't allowed anymore. So, I snuck onto the back while he was at someone's door. I jumped too late, hand on the crate dragging it all down as I leapt in the air. Bottles shattered around me, slicing my skin, sticky sweetness soaking my clothes. Yet I jumped up and ran with my bruised pride, and I hid behind a bush, bleeding and ashamed.

When I got home, Mum didn't yell. She didn't ask if I was okay. Just looked at me with shame and walked away. It was like I was the mess, the trouble, the naughty one, and she was always covering and trying to clean up.

When I was eight, Dad filled an old pram with vegetables from the garden. My sister and I had to push it through the streets, knocking on strangers' doors to sell them. It was cold in the mornings but hot in the afternoons. It was boring, and my legs were sore. I hated every second of it, but I was used to doing what I was told.

One regular old man asked us in to rest. He was polite and smiled warmly; I thought he was kind.

But his hands were not kind.

He touched me in a way that made the air disappear. I froze again, mouth closed tight, eyes wide. I didn't scream. I never did. My sister was in the room, and I told myself I had to protect her. But when he chased her and locked the door, I couldn't move. I heard her screaming. Her voice echoed off the walls. Still, I couldn't move.

I inched down the hallway and saw everything. But I turned away. My body stayed still while my heart begged for escape.

When the screaming stopped, he gave her a lollipop.

We walked home; I told her not to tell. I told her he was lonely, that maybe it wouldn't happen again. I wanted to believe that; I needed to believe that. Because if it did happen again, and I wasn't there, maybe she'd be safe. Maybe I was the problem.

The next day, she went back. I stayed at a friend's house. It happened again, but this time she was brave and strong; unlike me, she told Mum.

The police came. I lied. I said nothing. I shook my head no to everything they asked about had happened. He lied, too, and smiled like nothing touched him. He walked away, free, and I stayed in silence with the guilt and self-blame. He hurt my sister because of me.

At school around Halloween, kids whispered about the creepy old man. They laughed nervously. I turned my head to hear the conversations and sealed my lips so the secrets could not be spoken. I looked away and wondered in thought if it had happened to others. But I didn't ask; I never could or would. By then, silence was the only thing I truly knew how to do.

Because silence, cold, heavy, and suffocating, had always been safer than the truth.

Chapter 4: When Growing Up Was a Warning, not a Wish

Poem: "The Girl Who Grew Too Soon"

They laughed in groups, their hands full of joy,

while I sat silent, shoulders tight, eyes to the ground.

Girls wore glitter and secrets and smiles.

I wore shame like skin I couldn't shed.

The boys let me be.

No gossip, no stares, just space to breathe.

While they smoked, I stayed still,

watching the world from behind a brick wall.

My dad's hands rewrote my body into a battlefield.

He called me fat and left me hollow,

a quiet war between hunger and the mirror,

starving to feel small enough to disappear.

Mum played pretend, cool and careless.

Parties in our room, vodka in mugs,

buckets full of sickness and laughter I didn't feel.

I froze. Always.

Even when I wanted to run,

fear rooted me where I stood.

My voice screamed. I swallowed silence.

And when the world gave no exit,

I made one myself.

I didn't leave because I was brave.

I left because I had to,

Survival was my plan.

"I didn't grow into a teenager I unravelled into one. The years that should have been reckless and fun were stolen by secrets, betrayals, and survival."

Starting high school wasn't just a transition, it was a severing. I left behind the small local primary school where, despite the pain, I was familiar. I boarded a bus each morning, one that carried kids from the local public and private schools.

It was supposed to take me somewhere new, somewhere better. But before I even reached the gates of that high school, I was already marked.

It happened on the bus. Private school kids with polished shoes and loud mouths leant over the seat in front of me. "Rags and dags," they called me. Then came the whisper that cut deeper than all the others, that my parents were cousins.

I didn't want to believe them. It felt too disgusting, too cruel. I went home and asked Dad, the one I trusted more. He looked away as he said it was true. Their mothers were sisters; that made my parents first cousins.

I didn't know where to put that kind of truth. It sat in me like something sour, rotting. I didn't tell anyone; I was a product of what I felt was incest. I just carried the weight of it in silence. It festered, it made me ashamed of where I came from, even though I had no say in it.

High school itself was a blur of isolation. I was painfully quiet, never spoken, not because I didn't have thoughts, but because I had too many and I didn't fit in.

I was bullied for my pencil case, the one with my name carefully printed on it. For my neat books, for trying too hard, for being too invisible and too different. But I didn't know how else to be, how to be a teen. I felt too mature to be one of them.

I didn't hear most of what the teachers said. My brain was too busy elsewhere. I zoned out constantly, trapped in spirals of thought that took me far away from the classroom. I lived in my head, a head full of noise and chaos and memories I didn't know how to escape.

But somehow, I taught myself. I learnt how to solve equations, how to write essays, how to make things make sense. Math especially—I clung to it like a lifeline. It had rules. Logic. Predictability and problem-solving and was great at consuming my time. I didn't need to ask for help, and I didn't want to. "Can you repeat that, sir?" was never going to leave my lips. I'd figure it out myself like I always do. The black-and-white certainty of math was soothing when everything else in my life was grey.

I made a few friends, but they were more like acquaintances. I was the helper, the tutor, the one who did the homework or showed them how. It made me feel useful, maybe even smart. Like I had value beyond the things I couldn't speak about. But deep down, I knew they wouldn't have noticed if I disappeared; I was just someone to get their work done for them.

At lunch, I sat with the boys—not because I was one of them, but because they didn't care if I sat in silence. They weren't bitchy.

They didn't expect me to gossip or look perfect. They smoked; I kept a lookout. I felt like an outsider standing just close enough to feel included. I never followed, but that was because, to me, being different was way cooler. I was the girl with no makeup, no brand names, just silence and space. They gave me that, plus safety. I felt I found my place.

I envied the other girls—their laughter, their glossy hair, their casual ease. But I also feared it because the way they touched each other's arms, what did that mean? They whispered in circles I was never invited into. What did they say, and how did they speak so freely too? I didn't know how to be soft like that; I didn't know how to be a girl who was carefree, chilled out without a care in the world.

The Blue Light Discos were my first taste of freedom. Loud music, coloured lights, the promise of something ordinary. Alcohol, always alcohol—my older cousin could buy it for us. Strongbow's, cask wine, cheap vodka, anything that made the edges blur. We drank in parks before heading to the disco, hidden behind toilet blocks, shivering in the cold as we passed around bottles. The alcohol made me forget; it turned down the volume in my head. I laughed, I danced, I pretended my real life didn't exist.

Mum didn't always approve. Some nights she'd say no. But the window became my escape hatch. My sister would approve and be my alibi; she would close the window behind me as I took the steep drop outside. I'd slip out into the night like a shadow, heart racing with the thrill of it. Disobedience didn't scare me—staying in did. Staying meant being watched, being used, being yelled at and violated. Out there, I could breathe. To return, I tapped on the side of the house; my sister would open the back door and let me back in.

Mum changed too. She stopped caring about where I was or what I did. Instead, she shifted her energy to my friends. She became their "cool mum," the one who let everyone drink, who smiled and encouraged us to stay up late. She played the role of hostess, laughing too loudly, sharing made-up stories that made people laugh out loud, while I sat uncomfortable, silenced in the crowd.

It wasn't for me; it never had been. It was always about how others saw her. I was still the invisible, unloved, unwanted child.

Weekends became chaotic. Sleepovers, hangovers, buckets filled with vomit. Rooms thick with the stench of stale alcohol and unspoken regrets. But in the mess, I felt something that almost resembled belonging. I wasn't happy, but I was included—and for once, liked by someone.

Then my dad changed. Or maybe he didn't. Maybe I just started to see it. The looks, the comments, the accidental brushes, and the way his hand would linger too long. Then one night, it went further. His pants were down. Mine were taken off, but I froze completely. I was in shock. I stared at the wall and left my body. My breath got caught in my throat and stayed there silently.

He told me I was getting fat.

The words seared through me more than his touch. Fat, ugly, unwanted—I had to fix that. I stopped eating. I started skipping meals, hiding food, pretending I was full. I weighed myself constantly. I wanted to disappear, and I thought if I was small enough, maybe I could.

Eventually, I told the school counsellor. I walked in with shaking hands and a cracking voice and told her everything— the eating, the abuse, the fear. She nodded, she took notes, then she disappeared.

She called my parents and had a meeting telling them everything. They, of course, just denied everything. The trouble I got in when they came home, for the lies I told on them, the beating—black and blue, silenced once again.

Everything exploded. My secrets weren't secrets anymore. But no one fixed it, no one made it stop. Instead, my body gave in. I became gaunt; my clothes hung off me, my periods stopped, and I began fainting. People stared, but no one really cared or saw the reason why.

Still, he told me I was fat.

Then I met James. He was twenty-one, a DJ, and so different from everyone I knew. He didn't touch me; he held me. I would curl into him like I was trying to disappear into his skin. It wasn't love, not really. But it was safety, it was quiet, it was warm, and it always made me sleepy.

Mum liked him. Too much. She encouraged him to sleep over. She started acting strange, making us pose with the neighbour's grandchild, trying to stage photos of us that looked provocative. She joked about babies, about getting pregnant young—it made me feel sick. She wanted grandkids, yet not her own daughter. She wanted someone to mold into a mother so she could perform as a grandmother.

Meanwhile, my brother started bonding with James. They'd drink together, play games at the arcade, act like everything was normal. While they were out, the abuse would return from Dad's hands. His words, his shame—I learnt to hide in plain sight.

I'd had enough, and a great plan came to my mind. I asked James to marry me. I didn't love him; I wasn't even sure I knew what love was. But I believed that if I could move out, get engaged, start a new life—maybe, just maybe, I could finally be safe, and that would be enough.

He said yes.

I packed everything I could into a bag—Notebooks, Clothes, Toothbrush—and took all my Secrets with me. I didn't look back; I didn't want to turn. I wanted this whole childhood to just be gone.

We moved in together. A small old house out by the sea, nothing special, old and run down, but I was free. It had a locked door; it didn't smell like beer or fear. No one watched me sleep. No one barged in. It was imperfect, it was unstable, but it was mine.

For the first time, I felt the weight of the past loosen just slightly. I didn't know how to heal, but I knew how to escape—and sometimes, that's the first step toward surviving.

And in those quiet nights, wrapped in blankets instead of shame, I dreamt not of love but of freedom—the only thing I had ever truly wanted. The only sad thing I missed was I had to give up school to have my new life.

Reflection: - Lived Experience of Child Sexual Abuse

Through my book, you will have read that there were four perpetrators of child sexual abuse in my life. Each one silenced me in a different way, yet all left the same wound: silence, shame, and stolen safety.

As the older sister, I believed it was my role to protect my younger sister. I watched her fight, run, and report. Her voice was loud where mine was quiet. She managed to speak up, while I withheld, denied, and in my silence, I unintentionally protected those who harmed us. Instead of being her ally, I froze. That paralysis carved guilt deep into me, planting the belief that I had failed her. For decades I carried the unbearable weight of *what if I had…?* What if I had screamed, fought, or told?

But therapy gave me space to see the truth: I was a child. I wasn't responsible. They were adults, and it was their responsibility to protect, to stop, to choose differently. They chose to harm. The shame was never mine to carry.

My freeze response wasn't weakness, it was survival. My body knew what my voice could not yet speak: stay still, stay silent, stay alive. That was my child-self protecting me in the only way she knew how.

The deepest wound wasn't only the abuse itself, but the betrayal. The very people who should have cared, believed, and protected were the ones who silenced or abandoned me. When safety is stolen at the core, trust in the world collapses.

Healing has not meant erasing the past, I cannot undo what was done. Healing for me has meant reclaiming my truth. It has meant speaking words I once swallowed. It has meant slowly learning to believe what my heart already knew: I did not ask for this, I did not deserve this, and I am not to blame.

Even now, I sometimes still see the world through the eyes of that small, terrified child. When that happens, I place a gentle hand on her shoulder and remind her: You did nothing wrong. The adults failed you. The accountability is theirs, never yours.

A Journey Toward Hope

For years, I thought I was broken. What I now know is that I was wounded, but wounds can heal. They may leave scars, but scars are proof that the wound has closed, that life has continued, that survival was possible.

The silence that once suffocated me has become the very place I now draw strength. Where shame once lived, I now plant seeds of dignity and self-worth. The truth is no longer something I hide, it is something I own.

Child sexual abuse tried to take everything from me: my safety, my trust, my innocence. But it did not take me. I am still here. I am still breathing. I am still fighting for joy, for peace, for freedom. And that is something no perpetrator could ever steal.

Empowerment and Recovery

Reclaiming my life has been a slow, uneven journey. It has meant therapy, tears, nights of grief, and mornings of courage. It has meant unlearning lies and finding new truths. Most of all, it has meant discovering that my voice, the one that once felt lost forever, was never gone. It was waiting for me.

Today, I choose to use my voice. Not just for myself, but for others who are still silenced. I want every survivor to know:

- Your silence was survival.
- Your shame was never yours.

- Your worth has never left you.

You are not broken. You are proof of strength, resilience, and the possibility of joy after devastation.

A Message to the Child I Was

To the little girl inside me: You survived the unimaginable. You carried truths too heavy for a child to bear. You froze because you had to. You stayed silent because it kept you safe. And now, as an adult, I will keep reminding you: You are not to blame. You are enough. You are loved. And you are free.

Key Messages for Survivors and Supporters of Child Sexual Abuse

For Survivors

- **Your silence was survival.** Whether you froze, stayed quiet, or couldn't speak until years later, your story is still valid.

- **The shame and guilt are not yours.** They belong entirely to the adults who harmed and failed you.

- **You were a child.** It was never your responsibility to stop the abuse or protect others.

- **Your body's freeze, flight, or fawn response kept you alive.** That was not weakness, it was wisdom.

- **Healing is possible.** It may take time, but your voice, your worth, and your joy can be reclaimed.

- **You are not broken.** You are living proof of survival, strength, and resilience.

- **You deserve safety, love, respect, and care** then, now, and always.

For Supporters

- **Believe them immediately.** Children rarely lie about sexual abuse. Your belief is the foundation of their healing.

- **Stay calm and present.** Your reaction shapes how safe they feel in disclosing.

- **Never blame the child.** Abuse is never the fault of a child, no matter the circumstances.

- **Protect and act.** Ensure the child's immediate safety and report to the appropriate authorities.

- **Offer consistency and stability.** Safe adults help rebuild broken trust.

- **Respect their pace.** Don't pressure them for details. Let them share in their own way, in their own time.

- **Be patient.** Healing is not linear. Your steady presence matters more than perfect words.

- **Empower, don't control.** Survivors heal best when they are given choice, agency, and unconditional respect.

Final Message: "Believe, Protect, Respect, Support. Survivors of child sexual abuse heal best when they are heard without judgment, kept safe without question, and given the power to choose their own path forward."

Do & Don't List for Responding to Child Sexual Abuse Disclosures

☑ **Do:**

- Believe them immediately, your belief matters most.

- Stay calm and composed, your reaction tells them it's safe.

- Reassure them: "This is not your fault. You did nothing wrong."

- Listen without judgment, let them speak in their own words.

- Ensure safety right away, remove them from the abuser.

- Follow mandatory reporting requirements, acting protects others too.

- Offer ongoing stability and care, safety is built over time.

- Respect their pace, don't force details before they're ready.

✗ Don't:

- Don't ask leading questions, it can confuse or retraumatise.

- Don't show shock, anger, or disgust, they may think they did wrong.

- Don't confront the abuser in front of the child, it increases fear and danger.

- Don't make false promises like "This will never happen again."

- Don't minimise or dismiss, even subtle doubt can silence them.

- Don't delay, immediate action is critical for safety and healing.

Key Reminder: A child who discloses sexual abuse has shown extraordinary courage. How you respond in that moment may shape their healing for the rest of their life. Believe them. Protect them. Stand with them.

Chapter 5: Loved, But Never Known

Poem - The Ones I Left and the Self I Can't Find

I left her in the flames I ran from,

called it survival,

but all I did was shut the door

on a girl still burning.

Her voice found me years too late,

shaking, broken,

echoing the screams I knew by heart.

And the guilt bloomed like poison

in the hollows of my chest.

I saved others.

Or maybe I tried.

Built men from ruins,

taught them to cook,

to clean,

to believe

while I starved on the inside

from a hunger they never saw.

Each goodbye etched deeper,

every lover a lesson

in what I couldn't hold.

I gave them everything

so, I wouldn't have to face the nothing

that lived inside me.

Then came her

soft in her storm,

a mirror I never meant to look into.

She didn't ask to be rescued.

I saw the need from within.

And suddenly, I didn't know the shape

of my own reflection.

Was it love, or was it loss

wearing a new face?

Was I becoming

or unravelling?

I still don't know.

But I carry it all,

the sister I couldn't save,

the men I tried to fix,

the woman who held up a truth

I wasn't ready to claim.

And somewhere in between

all I've left

and all I've lost,

I'm still searching

for someone I've never truly met,

me.

"I left the house that broke me, but the damage followed. I called it freedom, but it was just survival dressed as love, and I kept loving people who needed saving because I couldn't save myself."

I couldn't believe I was finally free.

Fifteen years old, and for the first time in my life, no one to yell at me, no one to beat me, no one to rape me or scream in my face. There were no fists pounding through walls. No footsteps echoing down the hall like threats. Just silence. Just air.

The past was behind me. And for a fleeting moment, that made me feel light. I walked the streets with no curfew. I watched the sunrise without fear of who would be awake. I could breathe. I could exist.

The world felt like it finally belonged to me.

I was happy, or at least I told myself I was. I lived with James then. I cared about him deeply, but I wasn't sure if what I felt could be called love. That word always seemed too heavy, too strong, too foreign. I didn't really know what love was. I don't think anyone had ever truly shown me.

James was different. He was older than me but, in many ways, still a boy. He worked nights as a DJ and days in IT, but his mum had babied him for so long that he hadn't really been allowed to grow. So, I helped him. I encouraged him. I reminded him he was capable, that he could cook for himself, clean, believe in something, believe in himself. Slowly, with my support, he started to stand on his own two feet.

His family didn't like me much; I can't blame them. I was fifteen, a child really, in their eyes. But I wasn't going to be like my mother. I wasn't going to trap someone in a life of isolation. I encouraged him to stay connected with them, even when they judged me. I didn't care about their approval; I just didn't want to turn into the person I'd run from.

Living out of home wasn't easy. I had almost no money, no backup, no real education, but I did what I always did. I pushed forward anyway.

I signed up for an online diploma in childcare. It gave me purpose, something to wake up for, something to drown out the silence. It was meant to take two years, but I smashed it out in eight months. I didn't eat much, barely slept. I'd study all night, not even realizing it had turned to morning until birds began chirping and the sun had come up.

I did it. I passed everything, top of the class. I felt proud, briefly, until I found out the course wasn't accredited. No one would hire me. My dreams of working with children were crushed in an instant. All that work, all that hope, gone!

I took whatever jobs I could find—junior waitressing, fish and chip shops, scooping ice cream for impatient customers. The environments were rough. I was blamed for everything, bullied, ignored, discarded.

No one said thank you. Just, "Don't come back."

When I turned eighteen, James's best friend, Matthew, came to visit. He was broken and raw from losing his dad to suicide. His mum moved out of the family home; his girlfriend left. His world as he once knew it had shattered into a complete mess.

Something in me saw the hole in him. I recognized it. I had lived it. I couldn't walk away from that pain. So, I didn't. I vowed to help him through it and told him I was here to stay.

My relationship with James was already fading. He was on his feet now; he didn't need me anymore. Maybe he never really did, if truth be told. Maybe it was me who needed the purpose all along. I ended it with James and left him for his best friend. I moved in with Matthew to help him.

It was like hitting repeat on my own life: new partner as a project, to help fix and get them right. Matthew didn't know how to wash his own clothes, cook, clean, or budget. But I did it well, so I taught him. I built him up, just like I did with James.

Matthew's family ostrich farm had to close, and for the first time, he had to look for work outside the safety of his home. I helped him find a path—security work. He liked the nightlife; he was good at it too.

As he found his rhythm, my world started to evolve and move in paths I never thought it would.

I got my driver's license, and I found work packing vegetables on a farm. The hours were long and repetitive, but the money kept me going. People there were kind but curious, with questions like, "Where are you from? What's your story?"

I lied. Every time.

I couldn't risk the truth. I made up a past, a new version of me—one that was practiced and polished, believable. A life that didn't carry pain, blame, or abuse. A girl who looked whole and complete, someone who would fit in and be able to proceed.

Then one day, the phone rang. It was my sister. She told me she'd moved out of home. Just like me. She was free now, too.

Only her voice wasn't full of hope. It was heavy and wounded. She told me that Dad had hurt her too—that the same hands, the same twisted moments, the same dark silences had reached her as well.

I shattered. My heart sunk deep into my stomach, and guilt wrapped around me like barbed wire. How could I not have known? How did I let this happen? How could I have left her behind? I was so selfish, so blinded by my own escape, that I couldn't see the signs. I had fled and left her in the fire I knew all too well.

My mum rang too, saying, "Lisa's speaking this untruth." I heard her voice and listened to her rage, yet silenced and unable to confirm or speak up to the real pain. I let her rant and put my sister down, covered for my dad and all his filthy habits.

I hated myself for it. That guilt didn't let go. It gnawed at me, constantly whispering, "You failed her, you let it happen, you should've known."

And the only way I knew to silence the voices was to drown them, pretend it didn't happen, not now or ever.

I started drinking. I hit the bottle hard.

I had a lot more money coming in now, and with it came the freedom to lose control. I was out three nights a week, sometimes more. Bars, clubs, parties—it didn't matter where; if the drinks were strong and the music was louder than my thoughts, I was there.

Alcohol didn't just numb the pain; it transformed me. I became someone else entirely—loud, confident, wild, the girl who could dance on tables and flirt with strangers and laugh without fear. Alcohol let me breathe. It gave me words when I was too scared to speak. It let me be bold when I was breaking underneath, able to socialize and be with friends.

I didn't just drink to socialize; I drank to disappear. I drank to forget my sister's voice, the screams I would hear. I drank to forget the hands on my skin, the smells and pain I felt. I drank to forget the lies I told every day to keep my fake life intact. I drank to be free, not realizing I was building a new kind of prison.

Just when I thought I had found some sense of stability, it shattered again. Matthew, this man I had taken in, rebuilt, and loved the best way I knew how, cheated on me—with my best friend. I guess that was my karma.

The shock didn't even register right away. It wasn't just betrayal; it was a repeat of every lesson I'd been taught: you give everything, and you still lose. You pour yourself out, and people still throw you away. They use you up, and then they spit you out.

Maybe I never really loved Matthew, but I cared. I tried my best, and that mattered to me.

I walked away again, and like every other time, I didn't leave empty-handed. I carried the weight of another failed relationship, another cracked mirror, another version of myself who couldn't hold love together or ever be good enough.

That same night, I met someone new—a guy from work, ten years older, familiar, someone safe I already knew. We kissed in a club, and somehow, that made it official. I couldn't walk away; his name was Daniel. He lived with his mum in a caravan. He was thirty-one. Just like that, I was back at the beginning—a new project. A new person to build, a new story to create so I didn't have to sit alone, stuck in my past.

I got a flat; Daniel moved in. I showed him how to manage bills, budget groceries, cook meals. I guided him the way no one ever had for me. We saved, planned, and dreamt.

Then we bought a house together, our first home. We painted the walls, planted a garden, installed a spa out the back. It became a real home—something soft and safe, something completely perfect. Something I never had growing up.

We sold that house, flipped it, and bought another out of town on land—a rundown, off-grid mess of a place, but it was full of potential. I threw myself into the demolition; it was the one time I felt powerful.

I tore down ceilings, ripped out cladding with a crowbar, pulled apart walls like I was tearing down every hurt that ever lived in me. It felt so good!

I drove the tractor through the ferns and tea trees taller than my head, crashing forward with nothing but instinct and grit. His mates watched and joked that I wasn't normal. "Most girls don't do this," they'd say. But I wasn't most girls. I gave anything a go.

Daniel was a good man, in so many ways. Dependable, loyal, sensible, and a hard worker. Someone who wanted the quiet life, home, land, routine, and a job. He wanted the kind of normal that sounded lovely on paper, but I was 22, and for the first time in my life, I wanted chaos. I wanted fun, I wanted to be free, really, recklessly free.

Every Friday and Saturday night, I was out. Dressed up, loud, laughing, leaning on bar counters and losing count of my drinks. The girl who had once tiptoed through trauma now stomped across dance floors in heels that barely held her.

I wasn't drinking socially; I was drinking like it was a job. I didn't sip wine and make small talk. I drank to get drunk; I drank to escape; I drank to stop the screaming in my head. The ruminating, the guilt, the shame, the memories, the flashbacks. The voice that still told me it had all been my fault.

Alcohol didn't just help me cope; it gave me a character to play. Someone brave, someone free, someone who belonged, someone who spoke without thinking.

As the drinking deepened, my mask began to slip. I became phone-happy, calling people in my drunken haze. One night I called my mum's sister, an aunt I had been close to. I told her everything about Dad, about what he did. I thought maybe, just maybe, she'd believe me and be able to help me out. Her husband was a policeman; maybe this was my subtle way of asking for help. But she didn't hear me; she shut me down. Refused to listen, refused to believe.

I tried again, I rang my Dad's sister, my other aunt. I asked if Dad or Grandpa had ever hurt her. She said no; she met me with disbelief too, coldness, and denial of my truth.

Suddenly, I felt more alone than ever. The only one, the special one, the chosen one. Not in a way that felt lucky but cursed. While part of me should have been relieved that no one else had been hurt, the other part screamed in sadness. Why me? Was it real? Or just some twisted story my mind had made up? That's how they made me feel.

It couldn't be real; in fact, it shouldn't have happened, but it was. My sister had confirmed it, and that felt like my fault because I had left her.

Lastly, I told a friend; she reacted completely differently. She got angry, furious; she wanted to find my dad and run him down with a car. She believed me, but her rage confused me. I felt protective of Dad, as strange as it sounds. Even after everything he did, I didn't want anyone to hurt him. It was okay for him to hurt me, but I couldn't let someone else hurt him. That confusion rattled me.

And when the drinking no longer worked, when even the laughs and loudness faded into hollow echoes, I turned to people around me. People I knew who did drugs, something I had never touched. I begged them, pleaded, give me something, anything. "Whatever is lethal, please," I whispered.

They didn't understand what drove the desperation in my voice. They didn't know I wasn't asking to get high; I was asking to end my life. They refused, and thank God they did, because I wasn't seeking drugs, I was seeking an ending.

At the pub, I was magnetic. People smiled when I walked in. They cheered when I ordered shots. When I stumbled home with Daniel's mates, they were always kind. They made me feel safe, seen, protected, and cared for.

I didn't sleep with them; it wasn't about that. It was about crawling into a bed and being held, cuddled; that's what I needed right now. Just for a while, just long enough to pretend I wasn't alone and someone cared about me. Just long enough to feel like someone's warmth could undo years of being cold; I craved that hug that made me feel complete.

Daniel didn't understand any of this; in fact, he never knew because I couldn't open up and tell him the truth. He wasn't a drinker; he was up early for farm work, content with slow evenings and early bedtimes. He didn't want a girl who came home at 2 a.m. smelling like smoke and spirits, laughing too loud.

We started drifting; he wanted to settle, I wanted to burn everything down and dance in the ashes. He tried to ground me, but I couldn't be held down. Not yet, maybe not ever. Every time he reached for me, I pulled away. Not because I didn't care, but because he reminded me of the life I was supposed to want. The kind of quiet love I didn't think I deserved.

And maybe, deep down, I resented that I had built yet another person up and was still empty.

Then came Karen, I didn't plan it. I didn't even see it coming. I wasn't looking for someone new, especially not a woman. That had never been part of my story.

Karen was different; she was quiet, messy, and broken in ways I understood. People mocked her, called her a lesbian behind her back without even knowing the truth. She was overweight, lived at home, had no job, no real direction. She was the kind of person everyone avoided, but me it brought on curiosity.

I saw her pain, her longing, her need, and once again, I slipped into the role I knew best: fixer, rescuer, builder.

I started helping her, just little things. Listening, encouraging, giving her hope where others gave her silence or fled.

And somewhere in the middle of all that... something started to shift. There was connection, comfort, then chemistry. Then something I didn't have words for, but I knew this much: I couldn't stay with Daniel anymore.

Before I left, I did what I always did best. I planned my exit, I secured a new job, found a new place to live. This time an hour away, I couldn't afford to stay working alongside Daniel after breaking his heart.

So, I left. Packed up another life and closed another door behind me. I walked away with my personal belongings and took very little. I wasn't one for greed, so the house and its contents I handed over; I didn't want a reminder of another disaster I had created.

I moved to Marraway, by the water; it was cold, the kind that gave you chills, goosebumps, and frozen toes. I took a night shift job packing frozen food, working midnight to dawn. I told myself maybe this would be the thing that would settle me. Maybe this new life, with its cold mornings and unfamiliar town, would finally help me stop drinking, however, I found weed now.

Karen moved in with me, and she brought her habit. I was curious, so I tried it. I hated it; it made me paranoid, but a few cones, then it was lights out, brain off, and sleep would become a choice. Just like that, a new secret began. A new version of me took shape.

Karen moved in like a gust of wind, loud, unfiltered, full of need. She had worked alongside me, no independence, and no belief in herself. The world had already decided who she was: unwanted, lazy, hopeless, and "too much." But I didn't see her that way.

I saw her like I saw everyone before her: a blank slate waiting to be rebuilt. Someone I could help. Someone I could rescue. Someone who made me feel needed enough that I didn't have to feel broken myself.

But this time it was different; this time it was a woman.

I hadn't expected that, I hadn't planned for the feelings. The connection, the way she looked at me and didn't seem to judge, the way she made me feel... softer somehow. Seen, but not picked apart.

Still, I didn't know what it meant; I didn't have the language for it yet. I didn't know if this was love or a trauma bond. If I was falling into something real or just repeating the only pattern I knew: find someone struggling, give everything, and call it safety.

But there was safety, at least for a while; there was laughter in the kitchen. There were cold mornings warmed by late-night shifts and warm hands. There were whispered secrets and the relief of not pretending to be okay with men anymore.

The relationship didn't start with romance, it started with care, but somewhere in between survival and solidarity, it became something more.

Just like that, I had a new secret, not just the lies I told about my past. Not just the mask I wore to be fun and functional. But now, this, us.

I didn't tell people, not at first; I couldn't.

How could I explain something I didn't even fully understand? How could I say I think I'm with a woman now, when I hadn't even said it to myself? When I didn't even know what "with" meant in this new context? Was I gay? Bi? Confused? Just lonely?

The labels didn't matter, not then; what mattered was that I wasn't alone, and that felt good enough.

Like every other chapter of my life, this one came wrapped in unspoken shame. I still hadn't healed, I still hadn't rested, I still hadn't stopped running; I was just running in a new direction.

By now, lying had become second nature; I lied about my childhood, I lied about my parents. I lied about what I'd done and where I came from. Each new town, each new job, each new friend, I gave them the same polished story. A role I had rehearsed so often it became easier than telling the truth.

Now I lied about Karen too, about what we were, who we were. I didn't want the questions, the assumptions, the judgment.

Because even if I was learning how to care for someone again, I still didn't know how to care for myself, and in truth, I still didn't really know who I was.

Looking back, I can see it clearly now: Karen was another chapter in the same story. A woman lost, leaning on me to be her everything. Me, giving all I had in the desperate hope it would fill the emptiness inside.

She hadn't been loved right, either; she was mocked, dismissed, and belittled. I, once again, stepped into the role of teacher, provider, protector, but I didn't know how to protect myself. I never had.

By the time I looked up from the chaos, I was far from where I started, but still nowhere close to being whole.

I was older, wiser, maybe. But the lies I lived in still wrapped around me like barbed wire dressed as safety. The weed whispered promises of freedom it never kept. And my heart still beat for people who needed fixing, because fixing them made me feel real.

Karen was the end of another cycle. The beginning of something I didn't yet have the tools to understand. But for a time, I had someone, I wasn't alone, even if the truth stayed buried, even if the pain was still stitched into my skin... I had carved a life out of nothing.

I had kept going.

Chapter 6: Waves of Change

Poem: The Girl by the Sea

I came to the sea with my hands half-broken,

My heart a mosaic of silence and scars.

I stood in the wind, hollow and hoping,

Wishing the waves would wash who we are.

Midnight shifts and empty hallways,

The clang of trolleys and fists I couldn't fight.

Tears in the shower, breath caught in panic

Each sunrise a battle just to survive the night.

I wore a smile stitched from silence,

Played mother to children not mine to keep.

Their laughter gave rhythm to my aching spirit,

Their love pulled me up from the dark and deep.

Tiny coffins, and goodbyes in whispers,

Eyes that opened just once to say "bye."

A grief so wide, it cracked me open

But still, I stayed and let the sorrow flow.

I wanted to be love, not just be loved.

To give what no one had given to me.

So I built a home with noisy laughter,

And raised a village by the sea.

Not every tide was kind or gentle,

Some days I drowned behind my eyes.

But piece by piece, I kept returning,

Learning which parts of me would rise.

"Sometimes the tide takes everything from you, and when it returns, it leaves behind pieces of who you're meant to become."

Moving to Marraway was like taking a long, shaky breath after years of suffocating. It wasn't glamorous, and it wasn't far, but it was far enough from the chaos I had come from, and sometimes, distance is everything. With every kilometer between me and my past, I felt a little less tangled in the weight of old trauma. It wasn't gone, just quieter, and that was something.

Our house was one street away from the ocean, just one. The smell of salt was in the air, and the wind always carried with it a kind of magic. Something about the endless stretch of water made me feel like anything might be possible. Like maybe I could start again, a fresh start.

I was with Karen now. I didn't really know what we were, not fully. I liked her; she was safe, fun, outgoing. People gravitated toward her. She lit up a room and seemed so sure of herself. I admired that. I wanted to be like that! She was everything I wasn't, and everything I thought I should be.

So I watched her; I mimicked her. She left her bong out once, and when she was gone, curiosity got the better of me. I tried it, just to see. I didn't like it; it made me choke, my chest tight, my thoughts heavy, and my limbs feel like wet sand. I couldn't move. I was paranoid; I couldn't leave the house. But it made me sleepy, and at the time, that felt like enough because sleep meant escape.

I started working midnight shifts at Pie Haven. The job was numbing, cold, mechanical, repetitive. I'd wake at 11 p.m., work through the darkness, walk out to the bright sunlight, and fall into bed around 2:30 p.m. The house was silent; the world asleep or working. My hours didn't align with anyone's life; I was either alone or asleep.

To keep my mind busy, I found jigsaw puzzles. I'd finish them obsessively, glue them, frame them, hang them. It was something I could control. Each piece that fit gave me satisfaction; it made me feel a little more whole, even if just for a second.

Eventually, I met Sarah and Nicole. They worked the same shift, and we began talking, then laughing, then hanging out. For the first time in a long time, I felt like I had friends, people who saw me.

But Karen didn't like it. She said Sarah was obsessed with me, "my stalker." Karen didn't really have close friends of her own, and she didn't like me having any either.

Still, I clung to those friendships. Sarah and Nicole became my safe places. But then they both became pregnant and left work, and I stayed, for two long years.

The bullying started slowly. My leading hand would yell at me for things I hadn't done. Her tone sharp, her eyes narrowed. At first, I thought I was imagining it, that it was all in my head. But then she started pushing trolleys into me, slamming them against my legs, pinning me to walls, to benches, to machinery. She did it with a smile sometimes, other times with pure rage.

I froze. Every time, I couldn't speak; I couldn't move. My body betrayed me, my knees locking, my heart hammering, my throat closing. I wanted to scream, to shout, to ask why, but I said nothing.

Anxiety crept in like a shadow. At first, it was dread, then it was panic. I'd sit on the edge of the bed every morning, trembling, my hands slick with sweat, trying to force my legs to move. My chest would tighten, like something invisible was sitting on it. I couldn't catch my breath. I'd sob quietly, gasping through it, afraid Karen would hear. Sometimes I'd crawl into the shower and let the water drown out the noise. I'd sit on the floor, arms around my knees, rocking, whispering to myself to just hold it together, to just get through another shift.

Eventually, I started calling in sick. I worked just enough to survive. When I finally got fired, it was for being unreliable; it was a relief. The bullying stopped, untouchable, but the truth was unnoticed.

No one asked why. No one saw. No one knew.

Karen moved on to study hospitality, three years to become a chef. But she didn't have time to study. So I did it, every assignment, every test, every written word. I thrived on it, something purposeful, something that made me feel useful.

Then Nicole gave birth, three months early, a baby girl, Melissa. Tiny, fragile, her whole body barely bigger than my hand. She was in the hospital, wires and tubes everywhere. I'd sit beside her crib, watching her chest rise and fall, scared each breath might be her last. I touched her so gently, scared I'd hurt her, tried to take the pain from her with my touch. I couldn't, but I tried.

We prayed, we hoped, and eventually she came home. Melissa was home for six months before she was then given a second blow: diagnosed with cancer; the disbelief and despair. Melissa had to return to Mooralla for extensive treatment.

I gave Nicole breaks. I stepped in and watched Melissa closely. I promised Nicole I would treat Melissa as if she were my own. I held her during tests, sang to her while she cried, wished silently that I could take her place. I wish it were me who had to die. I wish she were pain-free and full of a bubbly, fun life.

We prayed, we hoped, and still, the news came: there was nothing more they could do.

We threw her an early birthday party, one last celebration. I stayed late to help clean up, desperate to stay close. Melissa was medicated for pain, barely responsive. But at one moment, as I held her in my arms, she opened her eyes wide, deep and clear, and looked straight at me.

It was like the world paused. Like time held its breath.

I don't know what she was trying to say, if it was goodbye, or if she was asking me to let her go. But it broke me open.

She died that night. Quietly. Gently.

Nicole asked if Sarah and I would read a verse at her funeral. I had never been to one. Not even for my own grandparents. My parents never let me, but I said yes; Nicole needed strength, and it was the least I could give.

The day of the funeral came. We walked to the front of the church, past that impossibly small white coffin. My eyes stayed down, filled with silent tears, my heart felt like it might explode. I wasn't ready to say goodbye, not now, ever, and just as I reached the podium, Nicole whistled loudly, playful, breaking the silence. It made everyone laugh.

That was Nicole's way, reminding us that this day wasn't just about death. It was about love, about the light Melissa brought in her short time here.

Somehow, Sarah and I made it through the reading. We clung to each other's strength. That day changed me.

Life moved on, but I wasn't the same.

I became a nanny for a beautiful family with three boys, Ryan, Andrew, and Christopher, and two step kids part-time. Ryan was the smiley one, full of giggles. Andrew, the forgotten middle child, just wanted to be seen. He was wild at home but perfect for me. Christopher was demanding, entitled, hard to please. I did my best with him. I loved being a nanny; every park visit, every muddy adventure, every silly story; they filled my soul.

Sarah and I stayed close; our boys, Ryan and Joshua, were best mates. We started our own playgroup, joining playdates, feeling like I had found a place, a rhythm.

I was let go with two weeks' notice from being a nanny; the family sold their business. I was devastated; the little family I'd grown so fond of was gone, and I was left all on my own.

I knew what I wanted, children. I wanted children of my own, to love, to protect, and to raise how I wished I had been.

Karen didn't. She said no, so I left her. I knew I'd grow to resent her if I stayed, and I couldn't risk that. I'd had a taste of what real love was, the acceptance from those boys, the cuddles, the laughter till tears ran down my face. I needed it to be able to become whole.

Karen came back. She said she loved me and didn't want to be without me. She said she wanted to have a family with me, so we began exploring fostering. I took her back, believing she really wanted this too.

I started my own family daycare, and thankfully the children I had been a nanny to returned. Their parents trusted me, the children adored me, I was their safe place. I became their Auntie Mary.

I had a lot of babies, mostly under six months old. The babies slept a lot. So I walked the pram along the beach and whispered stories to the wind. When it was just the babies, I missed the chaos, I missed the laughter, I missed the interaction. Eventually, I got toddlers, and the mess returned, the noise, the life I had grown to love.

It filled my home, and my heart.

For the first time in a long time, I felt like I was becoming the person I was always meant to be.

Reflection Lived Experience: Sexuality and Identity

For many years, I thought I understood who I was. I had only dated men, so I assumed that was the whole story. But then I found myself in a relationship with a woman, and suddenly everything I thought I knew about myself felt uncertain. I asked myself: What does this mean? Who am I now?

I looked hard at labels, trying to fit into a box I could understand, hoping it would make me feel safe. I was scared to tell anyone, even those closest to me. I hid my relationships, avoided using pronouns or defining my partner, and sheltered myself behind masks of normality. Shame and confusion sat heavily on my shoulders. I questioned everything about myself for years, lost in my identity, afraid of rejection, afraid of judgment.

Looking back, I see how much I carried, the fear, the self-doubt, the constant second-guessing. I wish I had known then what I know now: labels don't matter. What matters is your happiness, your truth, your authenticity. I am who I am meant to be, and other people's opinions are theirs; they have no power over my self-worth.

Over time, I learnt to go with the flow, to do what feels right for me, and to honor every part of my identity. I met wonderful trans and queer people who taught me through their openness, warmth, and courage that being true to yourself is what truly counts. They showed me that gender, labels, and societal expectations are secondary to living authentically.

I have learnt to embrace self-compassion and acceptance, to shed guilt and shame, and to celebrate myself exactly as I am. Every part of my identity, every feeling, every desire, every truth, is valid. I am perfect the way I am, and living in alignment with myself is the only measure that truly matters.

Today, I can say: being true to yourself, honoring your heart, and allowing yourself to exist fully and unapologetically is the path to freedom. Happiness, authenticity, and love, for yourself and others, are what guide me now. Labels don't define me. Being me does.

Hope, and Empowerment

Understanding and accepting your sexuality and identity can be confusing, especially when it doesn't match the story you've always told yourself or the expectations others hold. The fear, shame, and self-doubt that come from hiding your truth are heavy, but they can be lifted. Healing and self-acceptance are possible.

- **Your truth is valid.** Whether you've dated men, women, non-binary people, or everyone in between, your experiences belong to you. You are allowed to explore, question, and redefine yourself without judgment.

- **Labels are tools, not rules.** Words like lesbian, bisexual, queer, or pansexual can help communicate who you are, but they don't define your worth or your journey. Your happiness and authenticity matter far more.

- **Self-compassion is essential.** Be gentle with yourself for the years you spent hiding, questioning, or feeling ashamed. That uncertainty was part of your journey; it does not diminish your value.

- **Authenticity brings freedom.** The more you live openly as your true self, the lighter your spirit feels. Embracing every part of your identity, including the parts you once feared, releases guilt, shame, and fear.

- **Other people's opinions are theirs.** You do not need approval or validation to be real. Their discomfort or confusion does not define your truth.

- **Community can inspire growth.** Meeting open, courageous people, trans, queer, or otherwise, can show you what living authentically looks like. Their example can guide you to embrace your own identity without fear.

- **Identity is fluid.** You are allowed to grow, change, and evolve. You don't have to fit a static picture of yourself or anyone else's expectations.

Every small act of living authentically, speaking your truth, honoring your desires, claiming your relationships openly, is a reclamation of your life. You are allowed to exist fully, unapologetically, and beautifully as you are.

You are not lost. You are discovering. You are growing and, in that growth, you are perfect. The freedom to be yourself is yours. The love, respect, and acceptance you offer yourself will ripple into every part of your life.

Key Messages for Individuals Exploring Identity

- **Your identity is valid.** You do not need to fit anyone else's expectations.

- **Happiness matters more than labels.** Focus on what brings you joy and fulfillment.

- **Self-compassion is essential.** Be gentle with yourself as you navigate confusion, fear, or shame.

- **Authenticity is freedom.** Being true to yourself, regardless of gender, labels, or others' opinions, is the ultimate act of courage.

- **Growth is ongoing.** Identity can evolve, and that is okay. You do not need to have all the answers.

- **Community can guide and inspire.** Seek out people who embody authenticity and acceptance, they can help you see the possibilities for yourself.

Do & Don't List for Supporting Someone Exploring Their Sexuality or Identity

☑ **Do:**

- **Believe and accept them.** Honor their experiences and self-identification without question.

- **Listen without judgment.** Allow them to share at their own pace.

- **Respect privacy and autonomy.** Do not pressure disclosure or labels.

- **Validate feelings.** Confusion, fear, shame, and excitement are all normal.

- **Celebrate authenticity.** Encourage their self-expression, self-compassion, and growth.

- **Educate yourself.** Learn from trans, queer, and non-binary communities to better understand diverse experiences.

✖ **Don't:**

- **Don't pressure labels.** Avoid insisting they define themselves in specific terms.

- **Don't judge or shame.** Avoid expressing disappointment, disbelief, or disapproval.

- **Don't make assumptions.** Gender, orientation, and identity cannot be determined by appearance or past relationships.

- **Don't invalidate emotions.** Confusion or fear is natural; minimise it at your own risk.

- **Don't impose your opinions.** Let them navigate their journey without your judgment or control.

Key Reminder: Your sexuality and identity are yours to explore, define, and celebrate. Living authentically and embracing every part of yourself is the path to freedom, self-love, and joy. The more you honour your truth, the more your life can reflect the person you were always meant to be.

Chapter 7: Chosen

Poem-"The Ones Who Stayed"

I walked into motherhood

not through a hospital ward

but through quiet forms and case files,

with a partner at my side

and doubt in my throat.

They didn't ask if I was ready.

They asked for my story.

So I gave them the one I'd written

in self-preservation,

not lies, but longing.

The version of childhood I wish I'd lived.

I couldn't risk being turned away

for a truth too bruised to put on paper.

We were two women

asking a system for a chance,

not sure if they'd see family

or flag.

But they said yes.

And soon the door began to open.

Children came,

and left,

and came again.

And with each tiny goodbye

a piece of me stayed

with someone I may never see again.

I didn't grow into a mother gently.

I was thrown into the deep end,

bitten, broken, cried on,

battling red tape,

silence, resistance.

Not from the children,

but from the world built to "protect" them

while often looking the other way.

He called me Mum.

Not because I told him to,

but because he felt it.

He held me like home.

And in that moment, I became it.

My love wasn't soft.

It was fierce.

It showed up when the caseworkers didn't.

It fought for assessments they ignored.

It packed his bag when he left

and unpacked his trauma when he returned.

And all the while,

I was becoming.

Not just his mother,

but me.

A woman no longer hiding.

No longer folding herself

into language others found comfortable.

Not lesbian. Not bi. Not confused.

Not boxed. Just me.

Loving who I love.

Raising who needed raising.

Bleeding quietly,

but never breaking.

I was never their beginning.

But I was there for the in-between.

The becoming. The healing.

The first beach trip,

the first safe night's sleep.

I may not have given them life,

but I gave them back a piece of it.

And when the system tried to forget them,

I refused, I fort, I stayed.

"Family isn't always where you come from sometimes it's where you choose to stay, and who chooses to stay with you."

Karen and I had been together a while, quietly shaping a life in our own way. We were a team, in love as much as I knew love to be, sharing the load, side by side. When we began to talk about parenting, it felt like both a dream and a risk. Not because I didn't want children—God, I wanted them so much it hurt—but because I wasn't sure if the world would let someone like me have that dream. Someone like us.

We decided to explore fostering. We reached out to a local agency; they ran information nights and assessments and all the checks in the world. I still remember walking through the doors with Karen, her quiet strength at my side, and the tight knot in my stomach.

I didn't even know if they'd let two women foster. I'd never seen someone like us on the brochures. I'd spent my whole life keeping my relationship in vague language—"my partner," never "my girlfriend," never "Karen." I was always scanning for judgment, always cautious, always ready to defend or retreat. The words lesbian or bisexual sat like gravel in my mouth. Not because I was ashamed, but because they felt too narrow for something I couldn't yet explain.

Back then, I didn't even have the language for who I was. All I knew was that I saw people for who they were. Gender didn't decide my connection—it was kindness, warmth, the way someone made me feel safe. If I had to choose a label now, I'd probably say pansexual. But honestly? I'm just me, and Karen was my person.

The agency surprised me—they didn't blink. They welcomed us with the same process they gave everyone else: workshops, paperwork, home visits. It was exhausting, eye-opening, and deeply personal.

The forms asked about childhood, family, upbringing. I wasn't ready to hand over the truth of mine. So, I gave them the edited version, the fantasy I'd been telling people for years. It wasn't a lie exactly, just the story I wished was true. A childhood with parents who weren't broken, a home that didn't hurt. It was the version that wouldn't get me dismissed or labeled unfit.

The reason I wanted to foster was simple. I wanted to give kids the life I never had—safety, opportunity, someone who believed in them. I wasn't looking to be a full-time mum or a replacement, not then.

I wanted to be the fun respite carer—the cool, reliable weekend aunt who made pancakes and took kids to the beach. I was only twenty-three.

The workshops were full of older couples with grown kids. People who spoke in confident tones about boundaries and behavior charts. I felt different—younger, uncertain, and inexperienced. Karen was beside me for every session, quiet but present. She didn't say much, but her being there meant everything. I believed she'd changed her mind about kids; I believed we were in it together.

After six months, we were approved. Around the same time, I was still running my home daycare, juggling toddlers, nappies, bottles, and toy chaos. Then the calls started coming.

First were twin boys with high needs—they came for respite every second weekend. Every visit they arrived with heads full of lice—untreated, uncared for. I spent hours combing, soothing, cleaning. We'd take them to the beach, the farm, try to give them joy, only to return them to homes that didn't notice when they bled from scratching. It made me furious.

Then came a baby girl, placed because her mother needed a break. She had severe reflux and screamed with every feed. I pushed to get her formula changed, to see a pediatrician. The process was always layered in red tape—carer support had to ask DHHS, who asked the parents, who might or might not agree. Sometimes, she just cried until my arms gave out, and vomit was endless. I don't know how she continued to thrive.

Our house became a revolving door. Little feet coming and going. Babies and preschoolers, the age group I'd requested because I was terrified of teenagers. I didn't know how to reach them, or how to handle them, and didn't trust my capabilities to be a benefit to them.

Then came Jason.

He arrived with his two older brothers, Anthony and Benjamin, for weekend respite. They were split across two homes. Jason was only eighteen months old, and already he was shuttled between carers, supervised visits with Mum, then Dad.

The plan was reunification with his father, but things changed fast. His carer couldn't keep him—he'd started lashing out, violent tantrums, hitting other kids. "He's going home soon anyway," she said, so we took him.

He was supposed to be temporary. But temporary turned into weeks. Then months.

At first, I kept my daycare running, juggling other people's children with this little boy who clung to me and ran my house like a tiny tyrant. I put him into care one day a week just to breathe. But every weekend, he went to his dad's for transition.

One weekend he returned quiet, withdrawn, with a big egg on his forehead. It didn't scream abuse—he was clumsy and adventurous, always wearing battle scars—but something felt wrong. Days later, we found out his dad and partner had fled interstate. They'd left him behind, just disappeared.

The department shifted focus: reunification with his mum.

His mum was heavily pregnant; I drove Jason to and from visits. She was polite, respectful, and we built a fragile trust. When she had the baby, Mark, I took Jason to meet his brother. I let her have a visit alone—something I wasn't obligated to do—but I wanted to honor her as his mother. I didn't want her to feel watched like I had all my life.

Soon after Jason turned two, he was returned to his mum full-time. That goodbye broke something in me. He'd become part of our world. I hoped we'd given him love, security, a few happy memories. Then he was gone. I was lost without my shadow, and the house was silent and empty.

Three weeks later, a six-year-old girl arrived—Aboriginal, traumatized, and quiet. She came with barely any information; it seemed to be the common theme—carers the last to know vital information. Slowly she warmed to me and began to open up and speak freely. The things she believed were normal made my stomach turn. Her home life had been horrific—I reported it. The department confirmed she would never return home. I took her to the beach, watched her laugh in the sand, watched her be a child. That memory is burnt into me—pure, free joy.

Then the call came—they'd found Jason and Mark. I had a call prior asking if I would take Jason back into my care along with his baby brother, Mark. Three weeks they'd been missing, with Mum on the run.

At 6 p.m., we drove frantically from Marraway to Glenarra. I was handed a nappy bag, a screaming six-month-old, and then Jason ran at me with open arms. He hugged me like he never wanted to let go. He was thin, fragile, buzzing with relief.

We drove home to Marraway with him talking nonstop and Mark howling beside him. I sat between them in the backseat, trying to soothe two souls who had been through too much.

The next months were hard; I gave up daycare. Mark cried whenever he was put down, Jason was resentful, jealous, angry. He bit me when I didn't respond fast enough. He hoarded food, peed in his room, pushed Mark away. The department didn't listen, I begged for medical assessments and was denied, I felt invisible.

The little girl was still with me, but I let her go. I told myself she needed someone more experienced. Now I know I could have been that person. Her story mirrored mine, I see that now, I wish I'd believed in myself more.

Eventually, I let the revolving door close, I wasn't just a weekend carer anymore. I was Mum to whoever needed me, Jason and Mark started calling me that. Their choice, it made me feel chosen, Karen was "Kaz" to them, it suited her given that there was very little input from her.

Life became full. Playdates, tantrums, laundry, chaos, Jason was in kinder, Mark was walking. Karen's mum doted on them until her own grandchildren were born. Then we were sidelined, like the kids were replaced. She no longer saw them as "her grandkids," and she treated them differently. I tried to ignore it, even justify her actions, however, it was obvious to me and soon became obvious to them too.

My dad became unwell, and I mean really unwell. He was put in a medically induced coma and flown to Mooralla; they were unsure if he would make it. It was the first time in a long time that I was hit with a lot of mixed thoughts and emotions, together with the tough decisions to make. As power of attorney, the doctors were asking to think about the long-term possibilities, did we want him to stay on the machines or turn them off. My response was instant—turn it off, that wasn't the dad or man I knew lying there. But was that anger, spite, revenge speaking, or was it a clear, level-headed response? My mum didn't agree; thankfully, Dad pulled through, so I didn't have to argue or make that lasting choice.

I didn't know what I felt—love? hate? a tangled mess of both. I didn't want him to suffer, but I also did. I didn't want to regret not saying goodbye. So, I travelled the long distance and saw him. He was on life support in Mooralla, lying there lifeless and powerless. I stood there, fractured and unsure—was this karma seeking revenge, or was it the result of working so hard to care for his family?

Traveling from Marraway to Mooralla was tough, and with Jason about to start school in the new year, a decision was made to move back to Dunlara.

That move also marked a new beginning; Jason and Mark were placed with us permanently. A court order made it official; they weren't placements anymore. They were ours; Jason was six, Mark was four, Karen and I were legal parents.

Foster care had never been the plan to have an instant family, but love rarely follows plans. These boys weren't visitors, they weren't broken things to be fixed, they were our children, our family. So, we said goodbye to Marraway and the oceans that once grounded us and hello to a new chapter in Dunlara.

A place where no one knew our boys as anything other than what they truly were: ours.

I didn't grow up imagining what kind of mother I'd be. Motherhood wasn't something I saw reflected back at me in warm, safe ways. What I knew of it was control, silence, fear. Survival. But somewhere deep in my chest, even as a little girl, I knew that if I ever had the chance, I would do it differently.

And now, here I was, no longer the weekend carer, the "fun aunty," or the short-term safe house. I was Mum because two little boys decided I was.

It's strange how children can give you an identity long before you believe it yourself.

They didn't ask for blood ties or legal documents. They didn't care about DNA or marriage or titles. They simply called me what they felt, "Mum," and every time they said it, something cracked open in me.

There were no baby books, no soft landings. I hadn't grown into motherhood slowly—I'd been dropped into it. With trauma in one arm and colic in the other, I was navigating tantrums, night terrors, explosive nappies, court reports, and a foster system that was more interested in ticking boxes than hearing lived experience.

But in the noise of all that, I found something I didn't know I was allowed to have—identity.

Not just as a mother, but as me.

I began to realize how deeply I had spent my life shapeshifting, making myself palatable, safe, small. Always watching how I spoke, how I dressed, how I described Karen. Never saying "partner" too loudly, never letting my guard down enough to say love. I didn't know what that word really meant, not truly. I'd confused commitment for love, loyalty for love, survival for love.

But these boys—they didn't just need my care; they needed my heart. They needed gentleness, patience, safety. They needed someone who could meet their chaos with calm. To offer that, I had to find those things in myself. I had to grow into the mother I never had. I had to believe I was worthy of being seen that way and not make the same mistakes.

Some days I felt strong, other days I doubted everything. I wondered if I was doing it right; I wondered if I was enough. I still caught myself apologizing—to professionals, to schools, to strangers—explaining why we were a family, explaining the court order, explaining that yes, they call me Mum. No, I'm not their birth mother, but I'm their mother all the same.

Parenting kids who come from trauma is not soft work. It's fierce and tender and exhausting. It's being screamed at by a child who doesn't know how to ask for help. It's calming them down without taking their rage personally. It's knowing that the meltdown isn't about the spilled drink; it's about the thousand little betrayals that came before it.

Jason hoarded food for years—stashed it in pillowcases, in toy boxes, under beds. He'd take apples and bananas and hide them, not eat them. It was never about hunger. It was about fear, about not knowing if he'd be fed again, about not trusting the world to be kind.

Mark needed to be held constantly. If you put him down, he cried like his heart was breaking. He didn't know how to be alone, and honestly, neither did I. It made sense now why I always had to have a partner—a person to focus on, to try to fix—when I saw myself too broken and worthless to even try to mend.

Karen helped when she could, or when she was nagged, but most of it fell on me—the daily grind, the routines, the emotional labour. She loved them, in her way, but she wasn't maternal. She was about short, fun stints, then absorbed by her own selfish needs. While she stood beside me, I often felt like I was parenting alone.

Still, I found joy in the small things—the way Jason lit up when he saw his friends, the way Mark's chubby fingers curled around mine, the way they looked at me like I was the safest place they knew.

For the first time in my life, I was the safest place.

But the system didn't make it easy. I had to fight for medical assessments. I had to prove, time and time again, that my concerns were valid, that I wasn't exaggerating, that I wasn't projecting.

It wore me down, made me question my instincts. I learnt quickly that if I didn't advocate fiercely, they'd slip through the cracks.

I watched how the system dismissed certain kids, how trauma was overlooked if it didn't come in bruises, how children's voices were silenced under the weight of case notes and deadlines.

And I swore I would never be silent.

I may not have grown up with a mother who fought for me, but my children would.

Over time, I stopped seeing parenting as a borrowed role. I stopped worrying about whether I had a right to be "Mum." I was their mum. Because I showed up, because I stayed, because I held them when the world didn't, because I was there for the blood, sweat, tears—all the good, bad, and ugly.

My identity as a woman, as a partner, as a mother, as a queer person—all of it began to make sense when I stopped trying to explain it and just lived it.

People love boxes; they want definitions. Straight, gay, foster mum, real mum, biological, legal. "What are you?" they ask.

And I say: I'm just me.

I'm the one who gets up in the night when they're sick.

The one who shows up at kinder with clean clothes and snacks.

The one who wipes tears, soothes fears, and never gives up.

The one who makes silly voices in bedtime stories.

The one who stayed.

That's who I am.

A mother, chosen, built, not born—and finally, proud to be seen.

Chapter 8: The Ones We Carry

Poem: The Mother I Became

I did not walk the easy road

to find you.

I carved it,

bleeding,

bruised,

uninvited.

They told me I didn't belong.

Said I wasn't broken enough

to be helped.

Said love without a man

wasn't real,

wasn't valid,

wasn't enough

to build a life from.

But I built it anyway.

With syringes and second guesses,

with tears on the bathroom floor,

with borrowed strength

from women who held me

when the world looked away.

I carried you

through loneliness,

through silence,

through the wreckage of rejection

and the echo of absence.

They said I was doing it wrong.

Said I wasn't feeding you enough.

Said I should follow their rules,

feed their way,

feel their way,

fold myself into their boxes

and disappear like so many women do.

But I didn't.

I fed you with my body

and my will.

I rocked you with arms

that never once held safety

but still chose

to offer it.

You didn't come from my healing,

you came from my fire.

My fight.

My refusal

to be anything less

than everything

you deserved.

And when you cried,

I didn't flinch.

I rose.

Because your cry

was the first time

anyone ever needed me

and meant it

without conditions.

They said I shouldn't have tried.

They said I didn't fit.

But you fit

against my chest

like you'd always been there.

And now,

I will never

un-know

this love.

I am glad I did it!

"In a world that tried to silence me, I found my voice in the cries of my daughter, and in her arms, I finally learnt what it meant to be held by love."

Even though I never saw Jason or Mark as anything less than mine, there was still a quiet ache inside me, a longing that never really went away.

I hadn't been pregnant. I hadn't felt life grow beneath my skin.

I hadn't watched a heartbeat flicker on a screen or cried into a bundle of onesies or fed a newborn from my breast in the quiet of a 2 a.m. feed.

I loved my boys; they made me a mother.

But I hadn't yet lived the parts of motherhood that come from carrying a life.

That ache gnawed at me, not because I wanted more to love—I already had more than I knew what to do with—but because I wanted the experience, the fullness of it, the whole story. I wanted to give life, to carry it, to feel the shift of something growing inside me that belonged to no one else but me and this universe.

Karen and I spoke about it—long talks, late nights, round in circles. Eventually, and agreed upon, I decided to look into IVF.

It wasn't a decision I took lightly. I wasn't someone who could just go out and find a man to "get it done." Not because I was ashamed, but because I had boundaries and because I had trauma.

For me, sex had never been about intimacy. It was a performance, a transaction, a way to keep the peace—something to survive, not savor. My body, so often not mine. My voice, silenced in those moments. Every act felt like something I had to endure, not something I got to choose. Just another checkpoint on the internal list of how to please someone else and disappear in the process.

So IVF felt like the only path with integrity and control.

With a shaky voice and fear in my body, I contacted IVF. At the initial appointment, I was told that being "socially infertile" wasn't a valid medical reason to proceed. The law was changing, they said, but not quite yet. Still, they agreed to start investigating my fertility. If they found anything, even the smallest reason, I'd be allowed to continue.

It felt like being on trial, like needing to prove I was broken enough to be helped. If love wasn't reason enough, if being in a same-sex relationship made me less deserving of motherhood.

The process began; it was cold, clinical, invasive in every way—physically, emotionally, and mentally. Blood tests, hormone tracking, appointments. Then came the dye test— the one I'll never forget.

I can't remember its technical name, but I remember how it felt.

The room was bright and sterile. I was in a paper-thin gown, alone. A team of professionals stood at my feet—the one performing the procedure, the radiologist, assistants, and students. I'd said yes to them being there. I always said yes— easier to comply than explain trauma.

I lay on the table, legs open and exposed as they inserted the instruments. They explained what was about to happen, but their words were far away, background noise to the memories now storming my brain.

Flashbacks, silent screams. I froze—that familiar state I knew too well.

Not present, not in my body, staring at the ceiling as my past replayed behind my eyes.

Then the dye was injected. Sharp. Burning. Violent pain so vivid it pushed through the numbness.

No one at my head, no hand to hold.

Just clinical conversation and whispered instructions between strangers.

I heard someone say, "I won't see her again. Most people get pregnant after this."

And then, without thinking, "Just go home and have sex."

I blinked.

Have sex? With whom?

Did they even read my file?

Their words weren't just ignorant—they were cruel. They made me feel like I didn't belong there, like I was forcing something that wasn't mine to want. Like I was being punished for choosing a woman and not partnered to a male.

That night I cried for hours, not just because of the pain, but because of the shame. The shame they triggered, the part of me that still asked, "Should I even be doing this? Am I deserving? Will I ever be good enough?"

But the answer, deep down, was yes. This dream was mine to try—the chance to close a chapter and begin a new lifetime.

This was something deserving—a chapter I hadn't yet lived, a story I wanted to write from start to finish.

I don't know how I would've made it through if I hadn't met Kate.

We found each other in a closed local IVF support group, one of those online spaces where people shared in fragments—

heart rates, hormone levels, embryo counts, hope and despair wrapped around cycle dates and acronyms.

But Kate was different.

She didn't sugarcoat anything, didn't feed me toxic positivity or cliché pep talks.

She was real, blunt, hilarious, raw. She swore, she cried, and more importantly, she stayed with me for the whole ride.

I barely knew her, but she became my lifeline.

Where others told me to "just be grateful" or "trust the process," Kate said, "It's shitty, and it's unfair. You're allowed to feel every bit of it."

She understood the kind of grief that had no funeral, the kind of hope that became dangerous. She'd been through 21 cycles, back-to-back—twenty-one times she'd got her hopes up, taken the meds, bled, started again. Still, she found strength, and she showed up in my inbox, day or night, just to make sure I was breathing through the chaos.

She never judged that I already had kids. She didn't tell me I should "just be happy."

She got it—that this was about more than just wanting a baby. It was about healing a wound I didn't know how to name.

She talked me through every injection, every blood test, every meltdown at 2 a.m. when the hormones ripped through my body like wildfire.

She messaged me the day I picked up my first box of medication.

"Welcome to the circus," she wrote. "You're going to cry, rage, bloat, and feel insane. You're doing amazing already."

I laughed. Then cried. Because for the first time, someone saw me.

Cycle one came and went.

I did everything right—injected at the right time, ate the right food, followed the protocol like a soldier. But still, I didn't produce enough follicles. My body failed to respond; cycle canceled before egg retrieval.

Canceled!!!!!!!

Just like that—months of prep, thousands of dollars, and every ounce of fragile hope. Gone.

I told myself it didn't matter, that I'd try again. But inside, I added another mark to my growing list of failures—another thing I couldn't do, another reason to believe I was broken.

I sobbed to Kate that night, and she said, "It's okay to grieve the cycle. Feeling body let down and betrayal was okay."

Cycle two—I made it further this time. Retrieval, transfer, and even a faint positive line.

A phone call from the official blood test destroyed my positive view. Numbers too low—"nonviable pregnancy," they called it, like it wasn't even real.

But to me, it was. It was a pregnancy, no matter how short. That was a tiny human they had put into my body, and the pictures showed me so.

To them, it was a number. To me, it was a name—a future I'd already imagined, a baby I'd already loved.

And when I miscarried, I did it in silence, because no one counts the losses that come too early.

No one brings flowers for a child that never had a heartbeat. But I mourned that baby, the one I never met, quietly and alone in deep grief and sadness.

All the while, the debt piled up, no rebates, no public support.

Because I wasn't medically infertile. I was "socially infertile."

That's what they called it, like being in love with a woman was some kind of social problem.

Eighteen thousand dollars per cycle, savings blown, maxed-out credit cards.

No one understood my desire, not even Karen, but this was more than a wish, it was a need that I had to fulfill.

Six months passed; I told myself I was done. That it wasn't worth it, I couldn't do it again.

But the ache didn't leave, and curiosity was still there; that gave me inner strength to look at it again.

There was still one embryo left, frozen and waiting.

I sold my car, took out a loan, cleaned up the mess of my finances just long enough to try one last time.

Cycle three.

This time, it worked.

The second line on that pregnancy test didn't feel real.

After all the failure, the numbness, the trauma, it was hard to trust it.

I waited for the bleeding, waited for the phone call that would say, "I'm sorry."

But it never came.

Still, I didn't let myself celebrate; I felt guilty and afraid.

As if joy might wake up the pain I'd tried to put to sleep.

The pregnancy wasn't easy. I hated most of it.

My body didn't feel like mine—swollen, stretched, exhausted.

I developed gestational diabetes, I couldn't sleep, she sat sideways for most of it, stuck under my ribs. She was always in the wrong position, pressing against old trauma I didn't know was still alive in me.

But the one thing that made me smile was Mark. He was in love with my bump.

He'd rub it with his tiny hands and press his cars into it, giggling when the baby kicked them off.

He kissed it every morning, every night, spoke to her like she was already here.

Watching his love grow for someone he hadn't met yet made my heart swell.

He was going to be the best big brother. He knew it, and so did I.

Jason, though… he struggled.

He became withdrawn and angry.

Got into fights at school, hurting kids and stealing, and even hit a teacher. I tried everything to show him he wasn't being replaced, that he was still my firstborn. My boy, the one who made me a mum before I even knew what that meant.

But again, I was dismissed; the school said it was normal.

The pediatrician waved it off, "He's just a boy," they said. "Let him eat. Let him run. He'll be fine."

But I knew. I knew something wasn't right. I saw it in his eyes, the same kind of fear I once carried. The trauma, the rejection, not knowing who I was or how I would ever fit in.

I was doing everything I could, and still, I was losing grip.

The pregnancy dragged on, my body hurt in ways I hadn't expected. Karen offered no empathy, no support, just cold reminders: "You wanted this. You chose this. So deal with it."

As the due date approached, she filed for leave. Suddenly, she became the "involved partner,"

the one at appointments, the one the nurses smiled at, the one who was "supportive." But only when others were around.

I felt like a bystander in my own story. The only one holding the weight, physically and emotionally, was me.

The days dragged in the hospital—five long days of three failed inductions. Five long days of silence, of Karen pacing the room, coming and going between her phone calls and complaints. She wasn't sleeping there; she wasn't sitting with me, rubbing my back, or even holding my hand. She came and went, mostly asking, "What's taking so long?" or "Why haven't they done anything yet?"

I was starving physically, emotionally homesick, and missing my kids. My body hadn't responded to the induction drugs, and despite their repeated efforts, I had made no progress, no dilation, no signs of labor. Just a swollen belly, a baby lying sideways, and a woman crumbling under the weight of the unknown.

On the fifth morning, at 9 a.m., a doctor came in with a clipboard and eyes that didn't meet mine.

"You're scheduled for an emergency C-section sometime today."

That was it—no soft voice, no preparation. Just a decision made without me, dropped in my lap like a fact I should have seen coming. I nodded numbly.

When 4 p.m. came around, Karen seemed more anxious than me. Not about the surgery—about waiting. She huffed and paced, asked questions I didn't have answers for. She had eaten that day; I hadn't been permitted. She was restless, and I was frozen still.

They wheeled me away, alone.

In the operating theater, the lights were too bright, the air was cold. I was stripped of everything but my hospital gown and fear. When they asked for my weight before administering the spinal, panic blurted out a number 100 kg heavier than my real one. I don't know why I said it, just another symptom of dissociation, shame, trauma, nerves. But they didn't question it; they just dosed me up.

Karen entered, all dressed in scrubs. She was guided to my head, where she sat down. The focus and chatter were to the nurses in anticipation. I was invisible, just a piece of furniture.

My body went still, completely numb, but I began to shake. I couldn't feel a thing—not the pulling, not the tugging, not the slicing of skin. Just my own heartbeat, thudding in my ears like a distant war drum.

They worked quickly; I couldn't see over the curtain. I could hear voices, metal instruments, instructions, but not one word of comfort. No soothing tones, no acknowledgment that I was there, awake, and mortified.

And then she was out… Jennifer Hope, born into the world, tiny, screaming, fierce.

I tried to reach for her, but my arms didn't move. I couldn't feel them, couldn't lift them. It was Karen who held her first, Karen who kissed her, Karen who shared the news with the world while I lay shaking in a room full of strangers.

They whisked Jennifer away and took me to recovery. Alone again.

The one who had fought so hard for this moment, who had sacrificed so much—money, dignity, blood, body—was left lying under thin hospital sheets, trembling and empty.

When I was wheeled back to my room and reunited with Jennifer and Karen, Karen stood up and walked to Jennifer's crib, kissed her goodbye, and left.

"It's been a long day. I'm going home to bed."

No celebration, no handholding, no picture-perfect ending.

Just a sleeping baby, a room full of silence, and a mother learning how to breathe through the pain, physical and otherwise.

I watched too many movies. This isn't how it ends—your partner is there for you, loving you, and your baby in your arms together. The bonding together, the comfort and tears together, the strength in the love together. But that wasn't the ending for me.

That night, as I held Jennifer in my arms, her body curled against mine, I felt a kind of warmth I had never known. No words, no witnesses, just her little heartbeat and mine, syncing into something ancient and sacred.

This was how I met love—not in the delivery suite, but in the aftermath. Not in grand gestures, but in surviving what tried to break me.

After Karen left the hospital that night, it was just me and Jennifer.

I couldn't feel my legs, I could barely move. The spinal block from the emergency cesarean left me numb from the shoulders down. When the nurse handed Jennifer to me, I froze. I was scared I'd drop her, scared I'd hurt her. She was so small, so warm, so new.

I had walked into that hospital with the dream of breastfeeding—not because I truly wanted it, but because I thought I should. I thought that's what society expected of a "good" mother. Breast, then bottle—that was the acceptable formula, right?

I didn't want to be like my mother; I wanted to be the mother I had dreamt of. The one who would always try, who would be gentle and present. I had spent so much of my life being the opposite of what I came from, building a motherhood not out of instinct but out of refusal.

But now here I was, holding a baby I didn't know how to feed, mortified and alone. No support, no guidance, just two exhausted bodies in a sterile room filled with buzzing fluorescent light and silence.

I tried to breastfeed, fumbled; Jennifer wouldn't latch. My body felt wrong, my arms shook, my thoughts spiraled. The nurse took her from me and placed her in the clear crib beside my bed. When she started crying, they didn't help me. Instead, they took her away from me to the nursery.

It felt like punishment.

But even in the chaos of the ward, with babies crying in every room, I knew my baby's voice. Her cries pulled at me like hooks in my chest. I felt her pain; I needed her close.

So, I buzzed, I asked for her back, and something shifted.

Just like I had as a child, too afraid to ask for help, too stubborn to give up, I decided I would teach myself. I had brought nipple shields, tucked quietly in my bag like a secret weapon. I tried them, and she latched.

The moment her mouth sealed over the shield and she began to suck, tears welled in my eyes. I was doing it! I was feeding her! I wasn't giving up! I was giving her what she needed. I thought the nurses would be proud.

But when they came in and saw, I was met with scolding, cold judgment. "That's not the right way." "That's not what we recommend." They dismissed me, told me all the reasons I was doing it wrong, then they walked out, again leaving me alone.

I was left there, in the flickering dim of the evening, holding my daughter and wondering if I was selfish. If I was doing it for me or for her. Was I trying to prove something? Or was I being like her—my mother—defiant, stubborn, always convinced she was right?

But Jennifer was calm and settled.

She wanted me, not the bottle, not the formula. Me!

And for the first time, I trusted that I knew what was best.

We were discharged five days later. At home, I fed her the way I had in the hospital—with the shields, by instinct, not textbook. The health nurses raised their eyebrows. "Her weight gain is minimal," they said. "It's not where we want it to be."

So again, I spiraled. Do I top up? Do I force formula?

Was I starving her? Was I giving her enough?

I bought bottles, formula, and tried to offer it, but she refused. She wanted my boobs, not bottles, despite what the professionals had told me.

I pumped, I expressed, I filled bottles with my own milk. Still, she fussed. Still, she turned her head. So I gave her my breast, and she drank with ease.

My milk was enough. I was enough!!!!!!!

Slowly, she transitioned off the shields. We did it our way. I followed Jennifer's leads in what she wanted and when she had enough. Her happiness was all I needed to know I was good enough.

As I found my rhythm as a mother, I was doing it all alone. Karen withdrew; she clocked out. Her version of "parent" was a role she wore like a costume when the audience arrived. When the doors closed, I was left in the trenches by myself, my own battleground.

I didn't even have my sister—the woman I had babysat for, supported, stood by through eight children. The one I had doted on without question. She had her eighth child around the same time I was pregnant, a timeline that aligned with what would have been my second attempt.

She didn't know that part. She didn't know the pain I carried under my skin, the grief of miscarriage, the weight of silent loss. But one day, I opened Facebook and read her words:

"How can I be happy for someone who's pregnant when I can't have any more of my own?"

I froze.

She had a baby in her arms, a baby she loved, yet somehow my joy—my miracle—was too much for her to bear. And then she cut me off.

Just like that, I was erased.

She took my nieces and nephews, children I'd loved like my own, and vanished. Her silence was louder than any words. It echoed in the rooms I used to fill with laughter and lullabies. I mourned her like a death—not just the relationship, but the dreams of our kids growing up together, of shared memories and sisterhood, all gone and shattered.

I stayed silent. I didn't lash out, I didn't retaliate; I gave her the space she wanted.

And quietly, I sat in the corner of that grief and wept.

Because I knew how to lose people and how the loss never stopped hurting. Instead of ease, blame, and shame would turn internally to form answers. It's me!!!! It's my fault!!!!!!

Jennifer was the light that kept me warm in that cold. Her skin against mine, her tiny body curled under my chin. Her cries quieted by my arms alone, her trust so full, so absolute.

In her eyes, I saw the mother I was becoming—soft, strong, imperfect, but real.

Within her heartbeat against my chest, I finally heard something I'd spent my life searching for... love.

Not earnt, not forced, not feared, just love given freely, returned fully.

Reflection: - Lived Experience: IVF Journey

I went into the IVF journey naive. I believed it would be simple. I thought I would be pregnant on the first try, full of hope and excitement, ready to welcome a new life into the world. I didn't know then that I was stepping into a path lined with emotional turbulence, medical challenges, and deep vulnerability.

Being socially infertile made the dream feel even more precious. I was filled with joy at the possibility of finally becoming a parent, imagining the tiny hands I longed to hold. That hope carried me... until the first crash.

Failed cycles, miscarriages—hit like waves crashing over me, leaving me bruised and raw. The medications necessary for treatment carried their own burdens. My moods swung from sadness to anger, my body bloated and heavy, pains settling deep in muscles and joints. Headaches, nausea, and a thousand side effects became part of the journey, a reminder that hope and struggle often travel hand in hand.

I did it all in secret, wanting to preserve the joy of surprise if it worked, while enduring the heartbreak in private. The procedures were physically painful, emotionally draining, and sometimes isolating. But through it all, I met others who understood without explanation—people who, like me, were walking the IVF path for many different reasons. They were the only ones who truly got it, the only ones who could hear the unsaid fears and hopes, the ones who could validate the ache that words couldn't capture.

The journey taught me resilience in ways I didn't expect. I learnt to hold grief and hope in the same breath. I learnt to be patient with my body, gentle with my heart, and forgiving of my emotions. I learnt that it's okay to cry, to scream, to be angry, to grieve the losses along the way. IVF isn't just medical—it's deeply human.

After three cycles, I was blessed with a beautiful bundle of life. That tiny miracle embodied all the pain, hope, tears, and love I had poured into the journey. Every needle, every tear, every anxious night waiting for results was woven into the joy of holding my child for the first time.

I tried again for a sibling, enduring three more cycles filled with hope and heartbreak. When the cycles failed, I had to walk away. The emotional weight was too heavy. Sometimes loving yourself and your family means knowing when to stop—when enough is enough—and when it's time to protect your heart.

The IVF journey is not linear. It's filled with highs and lows, with joy and devastation often side by side. But it is also a journey of empowerment—reclaiming agency over your body, advocating for yourself, and honouring the resilience it takes to pursue a dream against such odds.

Key Messages, Hope, and Empowerment

- **Your journey is valid.** Whether it succeeds on the first try or takes multiple attempts, your experience, emotions, and struggles are real and important.

- **Emotions are normal.** Joy, heartbreak, grief, anger, and hope are all valid feelings during IVF. Give yourself permission to feel them.

- **Community is invaluable.** Sharing your experience with people who truly understand, other IVF patients, supportive friends, or online communities, can provide relief, understanding, and connection.

- **Self-compassion matters.** Be gentle with yourself. Celebrate small victories, honour setbacks, and recognise your courage.

- **Healing can coexist with disappointment.** Even if cycles fail, or you decide to walk away, you are not failing. Choosing to prioritise your mental and emotional health is a triumph.

- **Resilience is your superpower.** The perseverance, patience, and hope you show during IVF are acts of incredible strength.

Do & Don't List for Those Experiencing IVF

Do:

- Allow yourself to feel every emotion without judgment.

- Seek support from people who understand, including IVF communities or peers.

- Celebrate small milestones, no matter how minor they feel.

- Advocate for yourself medically and emotionally, your journey matters.

- Take breaks when needed; self-care is not optional, it's essential.

Don't:

- Don't blame yourself for failed cycles; fertility challenges are not a moral failing.

- Don't isolate yourself; even if it feels easier, connection can help process pain.

- Don't compare your journey to others'; each path is unique.

- Don't ignore your emotional wellbeing; therapy or counselling can provide crucial support.

Do & Don't List for Supporters of Someone on the IVF Journey

Do:

- Listen without judgment. Let them share fears, frustrations, and hopes freely.

- Validate emotions: "I hear you," "This is so hard," "Your feelings are real."

- Celebrate successes with them, even small wins.

- Offer practical support, e.g., attending appointments if welcomed, helping with household tasks, or simply being present.

- Respect boundaries around disclosure; not everyone wants to share their journey.

✕ Don't:

- Don't minimise their experience ("At least you'll try again" or "It could be worse").

- Don't pressure disclosure; respect their privacy.

- Don't offer unsolicited advice; IVF is medical and highly personal.

- Don't assume emotional reactions are irrational; mood swings and anxiety are normal under treatment stress.

Key Reminder: IVF is as much a journey of the heart as it is of medicine. Every step—success, heartbreak, pause, or end—is a testament to your courage, strength, and love. Your journey is yours alone, and through perseverance, hope, and self-compassion, it can bring joy, growth, and life in the ways that matter most to you.

Chapter 9: The Goodbye That Wasn't

Poem: The Day He Died

He died on Father's Day

a cruel kind of poetry.

The man they mourned

was not the man I knew.

They saw a father,

a husband,

a laugh,

a suit.

I saw a shadow

who crept into my room

when no one looked.

I saw hands that didn't comfort,

but claimed.

He died

and with him,

the letter I never let reach him,

the scream I never got to release,

the goodbye I never owned.

His mouth hung open in death

like it once did for lies,

and still

he took up all the space in the room.

My mother controlled,

draped herself like a curtain over the corpse.

She played the victim,

while I stood frozen

silent daughter,

holding my child

the way I was never held.

I didn't cry.

I didn't speak.

I let the doves say what I couldn't.

Let the balloons rise

like truths I swallowed whole.

They buried him with flowers,

with music,

with stories that never belonged to him.

But I buried something else,

the childhood he stole,

the rage I couldn't show,

and the hope

that someday

he might finally see

what he did to me.

And now, every Father's Day,

I remember not the man they lost

but the one I survived.

All the secrets that went to heaven,

and tight lipped, held withinside me.

"Some people die, and we mourn who they were. Others die and we mourn what they did, what they took, and what they left behind inside of us."

Father's Day.

The one day of the year set aside to honor fathers. But for me, it became the day I both lost mine and gained something else, a hollow kind of freedom. This year will mark eleven years, eleven Father's Days. Still, every year, I am thrown back to the phone call that changed everything, the double anniversary as the date remains the same but the day always a reminder through society, and publications or Father's Day celebrations.

It was early morning; I was still half asleep when the phone rang. My aunt's voice, tight with worry, told me that Dad was unwell and that an ambulance was on the way. I called the house. Mum answered; her tone was grumpy as usual. She said they were still waiting, but then, I heard him in the background. My dad, laughing, talking, making jokes with the paramedics. His voice strong. Stubborn as ever, he refused the stretcher and walked out on his own two feet.

They never hung up the phone, so I just sat there, frozen, listening. Was it bad? Or was this just another scare? It had happened before, three times, and every time, he had come home. So, I sat in disbelief, in denial, convincing myself this was no different.

Karen was getting ready for her first shift at a new job. I told her what was going on; she seemed oddly calm, not dismissive, but not present either. I called the hospital; they wouldn't tell me anything. I spoke to Mum again. While she was talking, I heard my aunt return to the room, and then, she said it. Out loud. Like it was nothing.

"He's gone." Gone? What do you mean gone? Where? Gone how?

The words didn't make sense. My brain refused to accept them. Apparently, he'd had a cardiac arrest when they tried to put him in a coma to fly him to Mooralla. Just like that, he was gone. On Father's Day.

I dropped the phone and collapsed onto the kitchen floor. Screamed. Sobbed. Gasped for air. The sound that tore from my throat didn't sound human. It was pain so deep it fractured language.

Karen walked in, fully dressed for work, and stopped. She didn't ask questions; she just knelt down and held me. Then she called her boss and asked for a few days off; he agreed. She packed for me, packed for the kids, took over everything while I paced and smoked, utterly lost.

The two-hour drive to the hospital felt like an eternity. I kept repeating the words: "He's gone. He's gone." Trying to make them real. Trying to push them away. Sending texts out to people and making Facebook posts.

When we arrived, I went to the nurse's station and told them why I was there. The nurse looked at me like I was stupid. "He's gone," she said flatly. She told me the kids should probably wait outside. I said no! They were his grandchildren; they deserved the choice. If they didn't want to come in, fine, but they deserved to decide. Mark (7) and Jason (9) said yes.

Jennifer, only two, clung to me; she didn't leave my arms. She was my tether to sanity.

We walked in.

He was lying there, mouth open, eyes shut, skin pale, waxy, too still, too quiet.

My mum sat beside him at a distance until we walked in, then draping herself over his body. Her performance began, holding his hand, swinging his arm, talking to him like he could still hear her, mentioning he was cold and pulling blankets up and tucking him in.

I stood there, frozen; every muscle in my body went rigid, I couldn't move.

His body, so still, and all I could see were flashes, horrible, piercing flashes.

His hand on my leg, his breath in my ear. The way his fingers would creep under the blanket when no one was watching, the way his eyes would scan me, the whispers, the demands. The pretending like nothing happened in front of Mum and others when he was done. His twisted form of fatherhood, a man who destroyed my childhood in secret and smiled in public.

The room spun, my head felt heavy, my chest ached, and still, I clung to Jennifer for warmth and comfort.

I never let him hold her, never once, not since the day she was born. She was always on my lap, beside me at the table, in my arms. My arms, because I knew what he did to girls, and that opportunity was never going to be given again. What he could do and what he had done were forever visions sketched in my brain.

My mother continued her performance, emotionless, rocking, hanging onto his lifeless body like she was the caring widow of the century. But where was this love when he was alive? Where was this tenderness then? It made me sick; it made me furious; this act made no sense.

I wanted space; I wanted to scream at his corpse. I wanted to say everything I never got to say. I wanted to tell him how he had ruined me, how he stole my innocence, how he made me feel dirty, broken, unlovable.

But I couldn't. Because my mother wouldn't let go of him, wouldn't give me even this privacy or moment to grieve alone.

So, I left. I walked out, trembling. My moment, my chance for closure ripped away, just like everything else.

My brother appeared later, like a ghost. He hadn't visited in years. Didn't call, didn't check in, but now, suddenly, he was here at the house. Walking through the house like it was his, talking about selling it, even putting Mum in a nursing home. He spoke of all the things they owned going to the tip, throwing away an internal life like it didn't exist. He was Power of Attorney after I agreed with doctors to end Dad's life support seven years earlier.

He didn't come to mourn; he came to take. He came for nothing more than personal gain!

Later that evening, Mum returned home. She rustled through the house with garbage bags, packed Dad's clothes, cleared his side of the wardrobe, tossed out the toothbrush. Gone, all of it, that same night.

I watched in silence, numb, disbelief, exhausted, confused, and cold.

This was his home, and she couldn't wait to erase him. How, so soon, please explain this to me!

I became her career, took over all paperwork, organization, repairs, and maintenance. Paid for the funeral, organized the wake, arranged the service, chose the music. Held my breath, cried in silence, strong and bold on the front, and supported everyone but suffered in silence.

At the viewing, I asked the kids again. Did they want to go? They all said yes, so they did.

He was dressed in a suit; he looked like a skeleton. That person there was a shell; that wasn't my dad. Not the man I had known, not the man who had hurt me. My mum had filled the coffin with photos and flowers, all her things. Nothing of him. Nothing that mattered, again more performance.

My aunt talked, my cousin stroked his fingers. I held Jennifer tighter, tried not to scream or say out loud what was the matter.

Karen took Mark outside when he broke down. I stayed, waiting, hoping to be left alone. Stared at the shell of a man who had shaped my entire life through violence, silence, and shame.

I felt nothing, no sadness, no peace, no release. Just numb, like the part of me that could feel had died long ago.

I wrote a speech, one I couldn't read. I handed it to the priest and sat in the back. Silent. Frozen, like a ghost in my own story. The speech revealed the narrative people saw and knew, not the secrets I hold onto.

The day of the funeral, I sat in silence. They read the safe version of my speech. My mum made a request to dig up her mother's ashes and bury them with Dad. A final family reunion. I found this odd and disrespectful, given she chose where to lay the rest. My grandma blew from the old resting place to the new as she leaked from the rusted container carried through the cemetery.

They didn't know him, so the eulogies were all wrong. They filled in blanks with lies, wrong names, and positions. Then, as his song played, he showed his presence, his coffin swaying and swinging; it moved relentlessly.

I swear it moved, like he was dancing, like he was saying goodbye, showing his humor.

I walked to the dove cages—white doves, I had ordered them. Said they were for his love of birds, but they weren't, not really. They were for me, for freedom, for peace, for closure.

We released them. The kids let go of yellow balloons, and still, I didn't cry nor feel any lighter.

Later, I stopped at the house to change. I found my brother was already there, in the shed, digging, rummaging, like a vulture, looking for anything of value.

Disgraceful. He didn't care; just like Mum, Dad meant nothing to them.

The days turned to weeks. Mum leant on me for everything. I researched a new home for her, arranged the sale, got her approval, then she changed her mind. Left me to cover the bills, the repairs, the insurance.

I did it all without question and at my expense—time, emotional, and financial. I always did.

She loved the grandkids, played the doting nana. But me? I was invisible. She never held me the way she held them, never looked at me the way she looked at them, never talked to or played with me like she did with them. Not when I was a child. Not now, not ever. And it hurt.

I let the kids love her, idolize her, told them none of the truth. Swallowed my pain so they wouldn't feel it.

Mum didn't stop her manipulative, selfish, controlling, toxic ways. Just days after the funeral, she was down the road, finding her next target, another cousin. Someone she barely spoke to, another twisted echo of her old patterns.

I don't understand how she operates, but I let her live her life. I always let her hurt me and stayed silent to my opinions and pain. Because I was taught that love means silence, that being a daughter means obedience, respect, and doing as I'm told.

But the truth still lives inside me and the goodbye I never got.

The scream I never screamed, the words I never said.

The moment at the coffin, where I looked at the man who hurt me and wanted to scream, "You did this to me. You broke me. You stole my childhood. And now you get to rest?"

But I didn't. I couldn't, and I wouldn't. Instead, I walked away.

Still carrying it all, and reminded, every Father's Day. I remember, not just that he died, but that he did when he lived.

Chapter 10: The Secret Life of Me

Poem: The Secret Life of Me

I crawled the floor in silence,

a shadow in my own home,

seeking truth behind a locked screen

because your eyes no longer met mine.

I found it

in words not meant for me,

in names you gave me behind my back,

in the soft heat you sent someone else.

And still, I had to play pretend.

Smile like a woman not breaking,

nod like nothing burnt,

mother like I wasn't unravelling

You saw my pain

and blamed the mirror.

I ran, not for escape,

but for breath.

To a house that didn't hold safety,

only history and hollow comfort.

You raged over the invasion,

not the betrayal.

You mourned your secrets,

not the woman you buried with them.

I split the life we built

room by room,

left you the things that once meant something

so, I could mean something again.

But even in freedom

I lived in hiding.

Lied about joy,

masked every movement,

let the children believe

what you wanted them to know

so, they wouldn't have to carry

our war.

You stalked my light,

called it unfit.

You cursed my wings

for daring to spread.

Still, I searched.

In corners and quiet,

I searched for the girl you silenced,

the woman you feared I might become.

And I found her.

Not all at once,

but in fragments.

In fire.

In forgiveness.

In truth.

I did not destroy the family.

You did not protect it.

But I…

I survived it.

"Sometimes survival means leaving without a sound, and healing means learning how to exist without permission."

At first, I thought the silence meant she'd changed. That maybe the storm had passed. Karen no longer hovered over me, didn't question every move, didn't demand updates, timelines, or explanations like she used to. I wasn't being tracked minute to minute anymore. But what replaced the control was worse—it was a cold, hollow rage I couldn't make sense of.

She wasn't watching me now because she didn't care.

Karen had become cruel, not in a screaming, throwing kind of way but in the quiet, calculated digs, the eye rolls, the way she'd glare at me like I disgusted her for even existing in the same room. She was always on her phone, hiding her screen when I passed. If I glanced over, even just in her direction, she'd snap, "What are you looking at?" like I'd violated some sacred boundary. The same boundary she'd never respected in me.

She would dress herself up, take provocative selfies in the outdoor pool. I remember watching her pose like she was in some cheap photo shoot, all while our kids sat inside, asking where she was, asking why she was in the pool when she wouldn't with them. Because that's just it—Karen didn't get in the water with them or anyone. She didn't want to be a mum, a partner, or even a person anymore; she just wanted attention from Emily. She wouldn't share a quiet moment with me, not in the pool, not on the couch, not anywhere.

What made it all worse was Emily, always Emily. Her "friend from work"—except it wasn't just work. They worked together, they ate together, she cooked her meals from the groceries I bought for our family and took them to Emily. I'd see it in little things—the effort she made for her, the way her voice changed when she talked about her. Yet, she treated me like I was nothing.

I told myself I was imagining things, that I was paranoid. That the gaslighting she'd done for years had finally rewired my brain to see threats where there weren't any.

But the knot in my gut wouldn't go away.

One night, I did something I'm not proud of. I waited until she was asleep, then I crawled—literally crawled—across the floor, heart pounding like a drum in my ears. My knees pressed into the hard carpet. I reached up and slid her phone from the bedside table with shaking hands.

I took it to the bathroom, shut the door softly, and turned the fan on to muffle any sound. I held my phone in one hand, hers in the other, and I opened the messages.

The truth screamed from the screen.

Erotic texts. Disgusting insults about me, cruel names, jokes at my expense, things she said about my body, my parenting, my mind. Words meant to dehumanize me, like I was some burdensome joke of a woman she was stuck with. But to

Emily, she was attentive, she was flirty—compliments, meetups arranged, provocative—she was hers.

I stood in that bathroom, bile rising in my throat. I took photo after photo of the messages, needing to capture it all, not because I wanted to use it against her, but because I needed to read it later and validate my own reality. For so long, Karen had twisted everything. She made me feel crazy, unstable, dramatic.

But here it was in plain text.

I slipped her phone back onto the table and crawled into bed, wrapping myself in the furthest edge of the doona like I could shield myself from her with distance. I didn't cry. I didn't scream. I just lay there, broken, numb, dirty.

And I kept the secret.

I couldn't let her know I'd seen the truth. I couldn't tip her off—not yet. Because I had to leave. I had to get out safely, quietly, without confrontation. I had kids to protect. I had to outplay the master manipulator.

So, the next morning, I made her coffee. I asked about her plans. I smiled when she joked about her "busy" day. I even kissed her on the cheek. I played the role she'd assigned to me—obedient, unaware, soft-spoken.

And when she left for work, I moved like lightning.

I packed everything I could fit into the car—clothes, schoolbags, essentials. The kids knew something was off, but I told them it was a surprise sleepover at Nan's. I didn't want to scare them; I wasn't ready to tell them anything.

And then I drove. I didn't even look back in the rearview mirror. I just kept driving to my mum's. I didn't like my mum's house, but I didn't have anywhere else to go.

When I got to Mum's, she was surprised by the visit. I, too, refused to tell her the truth. She liked Karen, but also because I knew I couldn't trust her.

I felt shame—shame that I'd stayed so long, shame that I hadn't listened to my gut sooner, shame that the woman I had built a life with had turned me into someone who had to live a secret life in their own home.

Karen called that night once she got home and realized we were gone. I didn't answer. I didn't owe her that. Instead, I sent her a screenshot of one of the messages—just one, enough to let her know I knew.

She didn't apologize; she raged.

Not about what she'd done, but about me going through her phone—her violation, her privacy, her boundaries. She never acknowledged the betrayal or the lies, just that I had "no right."

I knew then there was no fixing anything.

I told her I couldn't stay at my mum's. It wasn't safe—not emotionally, not mentally. The triggers, the clutter, the flashbacks of my childhood. The way she poisoned my mind. And it wasn't practical for my kids. I couldn't survive there for long. So, I told Karen she had three days to pack her things and be gone, that I would return with the kids after that.

While we stayed away, I kept the kids entertained with my cousin and her horses. I tried to create memories for them, like it was a little holiday. I wore a mask for them, laughed when I wanted to cry. Held my tears in the bathroom, pressed against the tiled wall, wondering how I ended up here and why I never deserved love.

When I returned home, I turned into a machine.

I took down every picture of her, every framed smile, every fake moment of intimacy.

I went room by room and created a 70/30 split of our belongings—I gave her the 30. Most of it had been mine anyway; she came into my home with nothing. But I wanted it all gone—anything that carried her scent, her energy, her shadow.

I even gave her items with meaning; if they had a story tied to her, I didn't want them anymore. I thought it would help me move on.

But it didn't. It still hurt.

In the months and even years that followed, I lived a secret life—a life that wasn't mine, not fully. I couldn't be open, because if Karen found out, she would retaliate.

She weaponized the children, told them I was bad, told them Emily was their real mother now. She'd bring them to Emily's house and plant seeds of confusion in their minds. She'd drive past my home to check if I was in, and if I wasn't, the phone would light up with calls and texts. If I didn't respond, she'd show up, unannounced, refusing to leave.

She questioned the kids about me—where I'd gone, who I was with. She used their innocence to spy on me.

If I made plans to go out on a weekend when she was scheduled to have them, she'd cancel last minute, forcing me to stay home, trapping me and ruining my plans.

So, I learnt to lie. I said I was visiting my mum. I said I was running errands. I avoided friends she befriended, avoided places she might find me. I told the kids the same stories so they wouldn't be caught in the middle.

I wasn't doing anything wrong. But somehow, she made me feel like I was.

She made me ashamed to exist in my own freedom.

I craved that freedom. I started to slowly rediscover myself— the version of me she had tried so hard to erase. I went searching for my identity, for my voice, for my womanhood.

But always, it felt like I was still tethered to her by guilt, by fear, by the damage she left behind, by the kids, who were the only innocent ones in this war.

Cutting her off fully felt impossible. The guilt clawed at me. I blamed myself for the break, for destroying the idea of a "family" for the kids. I felt responsible for the fallout, even though I wasn't the one who betrayed.

But freedom has a cost. I had chosen mine—not without consequence, but with truth.

Reflection: - Lived Experience: Domestic Violence

Domestic violence is not only about physical harm. It is a pattern of behavior designed to exert power and control, often in ways that are hidden from outsiders. It can be physical, emotional, or psychological, each leaving wounds that do not always heal at the same pace, and sometimes never fully.

Physical abuse is the most visible form. It may include hitting, pushing, strangulation, or other bodily harm. The bruises fade, the bones heal, but the terror of anticipating the next attack lingers long after the marks are gone.

Emotional abuse cuts deeper than flesh. Words become weapons. Constant criticism, insults, gaslighting, or threats echo in your mind long after they're spoken. These invisible wounds carve into the very foundation of your sense of self, creating doubt, shame, and an inner voice that mirrors the cruelty you endured.

Psychological abuse twists reality. It reshapes how you see yourself, how you trust others, and how you navigate the world. You start to question your judgment, your identity, your right to exist. Every relationship is colored by the past, as control and fear are internalized, making survival the focus, not living.

Coercive control doesn't arrive suddenly. It seeps in quietly, almost invisibly, until your life no longer feels like your own. Looking back, I can see how my independence was stripped away piece by piece until I doubted my mind, my worth, and even my right to exist.

At first, it felt like love, or at least what I had been taught love was. Gradually, affection became conditional. Every decision was questioned, every friendship undermined, every word I spoke measured. My voice grew quiet until it disappeared entirely. I believed keeping the peace, no matter the cost, was survival.

The lies I heard became truths I repeated: "You're worthless. You're unlovable. No one else would want you." Over time, I no longer needed the abuser's words; they had become my own. That's the cruelty of coercive control: it teaches you to continue breaking yourself long after the abuser has left.

Depression and anxiety wove themselves into every day. It wasn't just sadness; it was a fog that clouded thought, a weight pressing on every moment. Rumination became a trap, replaying every conversation, every look, every perceived mistake endlessly. On the surface, I functioned; inside, I was drowning.

Leaving didn't bring instant freedom. Coercive control lingers long after the relationship ends. Fear, self-doubt, and mistrust followed me into safety. Even in silence, I heard her voice. Healing wasn't a straight path; it was a slow, deliberate process of reclaiming myself one fragile step at a time.

Through therapy, peer support, and safe relationships, I began to understand something crucial: survival is strength. Seeking help is courage. Naming the abuse, speaking my truth, and acknowledging the stolen years is not shameful—it is reclamation. I have learnt that I am not defined by her control. I am resilient. I am worthy. I am reclaiming my life, piece by piece.

Domestic violence may have shaped my past, but it does not define my future. I have learnt to listen to my own voice, honor my boundaries, and trust my instincts. Healing is not linear, but it is possible. I can feel joy again. I can feel safe again. I can be whole again.

Hope, and Empowerment

- **You are not to blame.** Abuse is about power, control, and the choices of the abuser, not your worth.

- **Survival is strength.** Every step you took to endure was an act of courage.

- **Healing is possible.** With support, therapy, and safe connections, you can reclaim your voice, your body, and your life.

- **Trust yourself again.** Your instincts, feelings, and boundaries are valid and worthy of protection.

- **Empowerment grows from reclaiming choice.** You get to define your path forward, one decision at a time.

Do & Don't List for Supporting Someone Experiencing Domestic Violence

Do:

- Listen without judgment; believe their story, even if it is difficult to hear.

- Validate feelings: "What's happening to you is real," "It's not your fault," "You deserve to be safe and respected."

- Respect their pace; leaving or taking action can be overwhelming and dangerous.

- Offer practical support: childcare, meals, appointments, safe housing resources, or accompanying them to medical, court, or counselling sessions.

- Encourage professional support gently; share hotlines and crisis resources without pressure.

- Maintain confidentiality; their safety depends on the protection of their story.

- Be patient; healing takes time, and returning to the relationship may occur, but ongoing support matters.

Don't:

- Don't say "Why don't you just leave?" Leaving is often the most dangerous time.

- Don't pressure or force decisions; control must come from the survivor.

- Don't minimise the abuse ("It's not that bad," "Everyone argues").

- Don't confront the abuser; this increases risk.

- Don't make it about you; comments like "I would never stay" create shame and distance.

- Don't take control; avoid replicating the dynamics of abuse.

- Don't disappear if they return; continue showing care, not judgment.

Key Reminder: The most powerful support you can offer is safety, validation, and choice. Survivors reclaiming themselves is the ultimate act of strength and resilience. Healing is possible, even if it feels impossible at first.

Chapter 11: Some Friendships Don't Last Forever

Two Goodbyes

One goodbye came quiet,

a whisper slipping through hospital walls,

wrapped in pain you never complained about,

in laughter we shared too briefly.

You were soft in the way the world rarely is.

You held space for me when I had none.

And then, you were gone

before the morning,

before the tea,

before I could say, "thank you for being real."

The other goodbye was jagged,

loud in its silence,

a betrayal dressed as concern.

You stood with my abuser

and called it love.

You wrapped your cruelty in the word "help"

and watched me bleed through my birthday smile.

You broke something in me

not because you left,

but because you looked me in the eye

and said it was my fault.

One friend I mourn in quiet place,

with cemetery soil beneath my hands,

and stories only she would laugh at.

The other I buried in memory,

somewhere colder than death,

where false friends go when they show you

who they really are.

Two goodbyes.

One stolen by fate,

the other torn by choice.

I carry them both.

But only one with love.

A tribute for Jo

Forever a friend, missed beyond words, loved beyond time.

Not all heartbreak comes from lovers; some of the deepest wounds are carved by the people we once trusted to hold our pain gently in their hands.

It was my birthday, the first I'd allowed myself to celebrate in years.

A small step forward, one night where I told myself I deserved to feel seen.

Jessica, my longtime friend from high school, was coming up with her kids. I'd known Jessica since we were thirteen. She was loud, quick-tempered, and impulsive—the kind of girl who filled every room she walked into, whether you wanted her to or not. She had dyslexia, and back in high school, she'd copy my work, leaning over my shoulder and whispering, "What does this mean?" I tried to help not just with school but with everything. When her parents split, then finally divorced, I was the one who held her hand through it all. I remember the late-night phone calls, the sobbing fits, the endless need for reassurance.

That was Jessica—always needing someone to catch her before she fell, and I always tried.

She married Thomas young and had two boys. I was her bridesmaid; I babysat her kids. Even when life moved on, we kept in touch. Sometimes weeks would pass, but the connection always seemed to return, like it was anchored in our teenage years. But the cracks in her marriage were growing. Her life on the farm was wearing her down, and when she called me about coming up for my birthday, I could hear it in her voice—she wasn't just visiting me.

She was running from her own chaos. She needed an excuse to let loose, and I became the easy out. But what was supposed to be a celebration for me became a night she twisted for herself, and the damage it caused shattered more than just the evening. It broke the trust I had in someone I thought would always be in my corner.

I'd arranged a babysitter, Angela—someone I worked with—so Jessica and I could have a night out. I remember pouring us both a drink as we waited for Angela to arrive. I was exhausted from life, from illness, from the quiet grief of surviving things I still couldn't name, but I wanted to try. I wanted to feel something close to normal again.

We laughed like old times—the kind of belly laughs that used to echo through locker rooms when we were kids. It felt like a trip back in time, just for a moment.

When the sitter arrived and we finally headed out, I didn't expect anything unusual. We were meant to go to dinner, just us, catching up, reclaiming pieces of myself I hadn't seen in years.

But when we got to the restaurant, I froze. Karen was there, sitting at the table, waiting.

I can still remember the way my breath caught in my throat. The blood drained from my face; my stomach churned. Jessica looked proud of herself, like she'd just arranged some grand romantic reunion—like she hadn't just ripped open a wound I had barely begun to stitch closed.

Jessica smiled and said, "You need her. You've been sick. You're not okay. I thought maybe she could help." I wanted to scream.

Everything I had told Jessica about Karen's manipulation, the emotional abuse, the gaslighting, the control—she'd decided I was exaggerating. That I was the problem, that I needed to be fixed. Karen, in her usual subtle way, just smiled across the table like she was doing me a favor by showing up.

They talked around me, over me, through me. I tried to hold it together—to not react, to not let them turn me into the "crazy one" they were both quietly painting me as. With every word, every side glance, every loaded comment, I felt smaller and more invisible.

And then something snapped.

The pressure in my chest became unbearable; my skin felt like it was burning. The air in the room turned thick and soupy, like trying to breathe underwater. I couldn't take another second of their game or the interrogation.

I pushed my chair back so fast it scraped the floor.

Everyone turned to look as I rushed past tables, past waiters, and headed out the door. I ran through the cool night air like it could wash away the betrayal clinging to my skin. I didn't stop, I didn't look back, I could barely think.

I knew I needed somewhere safe, and in that moment, only one person came to mind—Jo. Jo was Rebecca's sister—Rebecca, who ran the back operations at work like a machine, always sharp, always in control. Jo had just relocated down from Queensland when I met her. She was rough around the edges, the kind of person people either judged too quickly or misunderstood entirely. She didn't play games. She had no filter, didn't sugarcoat a thing—what you saw was exactly what you got, and I respected the hell out of that.

She was bold and unapologetic, the type to tell it like it is, even if it made people uncomfortable. But if you looked past the bluntness, if you gave her a chance, you found someone deeply loyal, quietly kind, and fiercely real. She didn't gossip; she didn't stab people in the back. She had this way of standing in her truth without needing to be loud about it. Once you got past the walls, she let you into a softer side—a side that not many got to see.

In just four months, we formed a bond that felt years deep. It wasn't just about work—it was safety, trust, a friendship where I didn't have to perform or explain or earn my space. Jo just got it. She showed up—sick, sore, exhausted—and still found time to ask if I was okay. Even on the days she could barely stand, she apologized for not pulling her weight, and I'd just shake my head because her presence alone made everything more bearable.

She was one of the real ones, and in a world full of fake smiles and hidden knives, that meant everything to me.

Jo was a newish friend, someone I'd met through work. Gentle, quiet, funny in her own dry way. We hung out on the phone frequently or down the street; at work, we were inseparable. Jo spoke her mind and never mixed her words, so most people didn't like her. Jo, to me, was perfect—honest and loyal. Something in her had felt solid; she wasn't fake, she was real.

She'd told me where she lived, but I wasn't sure which unit in the small block of three. Heart pounding, I knocked on the middle one. Wrong door—they pointed me to the back flat, number 3. By the time Jo opened the door, I was half crying, half hyperventilating, half apologizing.

She didn't ask many questions, just let me in.

She listened while I told her what had just happened—how my own best friend had ambushed me with my ex on a night that was meant to be a celebration. Jo shook her head, rolled her eyes, muttered, "Bloody hell," and made me sit down. Jo wasn't feeling well herself—her shoulder, back, and stomach had been aching for weeks, and she looked tired. But she still showed up for me in that moment, as she always did.

From that night, Jo became one of the only people I could trust.

We worked together, and while she wasn't well, she kept turning up. She'd apologize constantly for not pulling her weight, and I'd just smile and pick up the slack. It wasn't about work; it was about being near someone who made me feel safe again. Someone who didn't ask me to explain or justify or perform, instead encouraged me to be myself.

Jo was tired all the time, sore, but she shrugged it off, said she was fine. But I could see something wasn't right—the colour of her eyes, the weight was fading away, and the pain seemed endless even with the pills she would take.

Then one night, she started coughing up blood. I remember the terror in her voice when she called me. I raced to be by her side. I called an ambulance shortly after I had walked in; she was barely conscious and fading. She was rushed to the hospital; they said it was a stomach ulcer.

She called me before they wheeled her into surgery. "I'll call you in the morning," she promised. I believed her, and I believe she meant it, but that was a call that never could happen.

In surgery, they found her full of cancer, stage four, inoperable. They closed her back up and moved her into palliative care. She died two days later—just like that—gone in less than 48 hours.

I didn't even get to say goodbye. I didn't want to impose on the family and was trying to process. I didn't know where my place was, so I stayed away in silence. I wish I had shown up and said one last goodbye. A chance I missed and can't go back to—not now or ever.

I was shattered; I couldn't comprehend how she'd slipped away so fast. We never got our morning chat. There were no long hospital visits, no drawn-out process—just a before and an after.

At her service, workmates gathered, the same ones who'd talked behind her back, mocked her, isolated her, and now they were crying, hugging each other like they'd lost a sister.

I sat up the back alone, arms crossed, eyes full. I could hear Jo in my head, swearing under her breath, telling them to fuck off. I cried through the music, through the slideshow of photos I didn't know existed, through the weight in my chest that hasn't quite left since.

And when they prepared to walk her casket out, I couldn't watch.

I stood, silent, then I ran—again.

I couldn't let her leave, couldn't make it real.

It felt like I was running from the truth. From another unbearable goodbye.

Even now, I visit her at the cemetery. I talk to her like she's still listening. I sit in the silence, remembering her dry humor, her courage, her quiet love. She wasn't in my life long, but she mattered and left a positive impact.

Then... there's Jessica.

When I came home the next day, she was still there, in my house, acting like nothing had happened, like it hadn't been a betrayal. Like she hadn't blindsided me on my birthday with the very person who broke me.

I asked her to leave.

She played innocent, claimed she was trying to help, said I needed support. That I was sick, that I couldn't see how unwell I'd become.

But her words weren't about care; they were sharp, judging, twisting.

Just like Karen, Jessica justified everything, said I was overreacting, dramatic, too sensitive, that Karen only wanted what was best for me. She mirrored every abusive thing Karen had ever said, as if they'd rehearsed it together.

She became cruel, vindictive, cold.

I saw her for what she was—not a friend, but a mouthpiece for someone who had already done enough damage.

She didn't know the violence I was still facing in my home, the escalation that was building with my son, the danger I was trying to navigate daily. She had no idea, but she didn't ask, she didn't care, she had made up her mind: I was the problem.

As I pushed her out that door and closed it tight, she walked out of my life, never looking back—just like Jo.

But unlike Jo, I didn't grieve Jessica with love. I grieved her with anger, with confusion, with a kind of hollow ache that betrayal leaves behind.

It's a strange thing, losing two friends so close in time—one to death, one to choice. One I would have given anything to keep, the other I had to fight myself to let go.

Chapter 12: nature verses nurture sometimes love isn't enough

Poem The Cost of Loving You

I held you when the world wouldn't,

called you mine when no one else dared,

built a home from splinters and silence,

and still, it wasn't enough.

They didn't see the bruises on my spirit,

or the fear behind my calm.

They saw a mother at the end of her rope

and called it failure.

But I never gave up on you

not really.

I gave you over to safety,

because I could no longer be yours

without breaking the rest of us.

And still they came,

with clipboards and cold eyes,

accusing me of being what I ran from

as if loving you through chaos

wasn't proof enough.

I didn't get to choose healing.

I had to survive it.

I had to watch you leave

with pieces of my heart still in your hands.

And in the end,

all they left me with

was a letter that said

"Thank you for your cooperation."

Like I hadn't bled for you.

Like I hadn't loved you

until it tore me apart.

"Some stories don't fit into simple boxes. This isn't about villains or heroes — it's about love stretched too thin, and the unbearable weight of trying to be everything for someone who could tear you apart in return."

Jason came to me at just eighteen months old—a baby still, wide eyes, clingy hands, the scent of institutional detergent clinging to his clothes. Jason had already been through ten homes in six months. Ten!

The paperwork warned me. It held disclosures, notes from two previous carers about violent behaviours, but I was young, naïve, and hopeful. I read those reports and dismissed them. I saw a toddler who just needed stability, routine, and love. I told myself they had failed him, that I would not give up.

God, how wrong I was.

At first, it was small things, attention-seeking in ways that didn't raise alarm bells. If I was talking to someone else, Jason would climb all over me. He couldn't stand not being the focus. I always let him. He'd curl into my lap, and I'd wrap my arms around him. But when the attention wasn't enough, he would bite—hard. His tiny teeth sunk into my arm. I told myself it was toddler behaviour, teething, and frustration.

I took him to a paediatrician. "Normal," she said. "Just a phase. Don't reinforce it. Ignore the negative, reward the positive."

So I did.

But then came daycare—pushing other kids, stealing attention, throwing tantrums that ended in him banging his head on the floor. Staff saw it, not me. He didn't do this at home, so I panicked. I was scared he'd hurt himself. I went back to the doctor. Again: "He's fine. Attention-seeking. Let it run its course."

He wasn't fine.

In kindergarten, he began stealing other kids' food—not eating it, just storing it. Sneaking into lockers, pockets full of snacks. I added more food to his lunchbox, even bought the exact brands he was stealing, hoping it would stop. It didn't. It was never about hunger. It was about control, thrill, and power.

In primary school, it escalated. He dug through bins, covered it up with lies to the teachers that he had no lunch. So every day, while he ran through the gate, I went to the office and handed his lunchbox to them. When he was caught stealing from a classmate's bag, he punched the teacher.

Again, I turned to professionals—a new paediatrician this time. Her response? "Maybe he has worms. Worm him weekly. He's underweight; the food won't hurt him." I left that appointment feeling invisible.

But I kept trying.

Every evening, Jason and I peeled vegetables together. It was our thing, our quiet ritual. I tried to talk with him, understand him, connect, and praise him. But the behaviours continued—more lying, more theft, more denial, and now violence.

He peed on his bedroom floor, called me names. "You're not my mother," he'd spit at me. "You love Jennifer more because she came from your belly."

I, without realizing, started pulling Jennifer and Mark away—not to punish them, to protect them.

Jason had started pushing Jennifer off couches, kicking and punching Mark. I'll never forget the day he gave Mark a black eye. And when I asked him what happened?

"It wasn't me."

Sleeping was dangerous. I would wake to him standing over me—sometimes a pillow over my head, a knife resting on my throat, or a punch to the stomach.

Always the same answer: "It wasn't me or my fault. You made me do it."

I got him into a psychologist. But he wouldn't speak. He'd sit and play Uno, eat the biscuits, and walk away when asked questions. He didn't trust them—maybe couldn't. So, we tried the school counsellor. Weekly sessions, gentle voices, redirection. He liked the attention; it calmed him for a moment.

But managing Jason became a full-time job. I built my life around his emotional needs. I let him sit on a pedestal of control because it kept the rest of us from being hurt. Slowly, the family fractured into two halves: me and Jason… and everyone else.

At twelve, he started running away. I would walk the streets crying, searching for him in the dark, begging the universe to keep him safe. There was a pattern—always on days that hurt: Mother's Day, Father's Day, birthdays, Christmas. I was exhausted, scared, alone.

I joined waitlists for services, parenting classes, pleaded for help. Nothing came of it, and no one helped.

The more love I gave, the harder he pushed me away.

He no longer wanted hugs; my presence irritated him. He told me I hated him, that I was the reason for his pain. Still, I clung to the story I'd built—that I was his safe space. He was acting out because he trusted me. Love would be enough. If I could just keep going, he would be OK.

So, I covered for him, hid the bruises he gave me, lied for him, protected him, even believed in him.

He opened the car door on the freeway—just a scare tactic, not really trying to jump, just control. So I returned him to the back seat with child locks, for safety became a strategy, not a comfort.

At skate parks, he'd snap if other kids outperformed him. Every bowling game he lost ended in fists and slammed doors when we got home.

One day, we had been out at the skate park. He was refusing to come home. He threw his scooter at my car; he refused to get in even after dark. I called the CAT team. No one from mental health showed up; instead, eventually, an ambulance came. They asked if he wanted to go to the hospital. He said no, so they left.

He had won again.

Then came the shoplifting, sugar highs, sugar crashes, fits of rage. Karen watched him walk out of IGA, arms full, no shame. My heart broke when she called me at work—not because of the stealing, but because the truth was revealed, because I didn't know how to reach him anymore.

I tried to teach him a lesson by having him accountable to the law. Karen took him to the police station. I wasn't trying to get him in trouble; I just wanted him to see there were laws and rules to abide by.

He charmed them—polite and innocent.

Karen dropped him home, and the fury started—with him punching me.

"I'm not your son," he said. "You hate me."

I asked if he wanted to leave, handed him my phone.

He refused. "This is my home. Just leave me alone."

Eventually, we resorted to notes, writing back and forth because it was the only way he'd communicate without exploding. On one Mother's Day, he ran away again, and this time we launched an SES search—helicopters with infrared cameras. He thought it was funny they didn't find him.

I was unravelling, my anxiety a mess. Out of desperation, I reached out to Karen—yes, that Karen. Begged her to help. She agreed but with conditions: I had to see her, do her favours, sleep with her, clean her house, and be useful.

I became a slave to two people with rage.

When Jason returned, I installed cameras. I wanted to believe his lies—I needed to. What I saw was worse than I feared. He was tormenting Mark—whispering things, insults, manipulation, the kind of language that reminded me of my own mother.

So, I called Mark into the kitchen, tried to protect him. Some days, I'd keep one child inside, the other out just to survive.

Then came the worst of it.

Mark had always been my quiet one, sensitive and thoughtful, just a boy trying to make sense of a chaotic world. But over time, even he started to shift. I saw it in the small changes—the edge in his tone, the worry in his eyes, the way he watched Jason like a younger sibling sizing up a storm. Then came the day I found out he'd been stealing—not out of rebellion, not for himself, but because Jason had told him to.

My heart sank.

It wasn't just Jason anymore; the ripple was spreading.

I contacted the police again, not because I wanted charges, but because I needed intervention. I needed someone, anyone, to see what was happening, to name it, to stop it.

Jason was taken in as an accessory. He sat across from the officers and complained about everything—the food, the questions, the inconvenience. He rolled his eyes, spoke with defiance. "Mark's got his own brain," he snapped, arms folded. "He chose to do it."

There was no remorse, no sense of impact.

The police were calm, professional, patient. Karen had taken them in, as I was home with Jennifer, and the police were too busy to come and pick them up. I sat at home watching the clock and waiting for my phone to ring. I watched the recording back later and saw the way he dismissed their presence, their authority, like they were beneath him. Jason treated the police like he was treating me, but without the use of a weapon or his hands and feet.

After the interview, Jason stayed at Karen's for two nights. I braced myself every time he returned—it was worse—and this time, he came back like a hurricane looking for destruction.

The door slammed open.

Without a word, he went straight for the bedroom. The picture frames were the first to go—glass shattering, photos torn from the walls, crashing to the floor. I stood frozen as he ripped our family portraits, stomped the glass underfoot, then turned and smashed one of Mark's dragon ornaments. He didn't stop—another followed by another. He was breathing heavy, red-faced, pacing like an animal in a cage, eyes darting between me and Mark.

He picked up a broken piece of glass from a frame and stood over me with it, like a threat unspoken.

I don't even know how I stayed calm—maybe it was fear, maybe shock. I didn't speak, I couldn't; my mouth was dry, my chest tight. All I could think about was Mark. He had to share his room; I was unsure of his safety in there and had to act soon.

The insults started—vicious, personal, and sharp enough to slice straight through my skin. I knew I had to do something, anything, to protect us.

So, I texted my friend, just four doors up.

"Please. Come. Now."

She and her partner arrived within minutes, and like a switch had flipped, Jason transformed. The moment he heard the knock on the door, the rage evaporated. He straightened up, even smiled—innocent and polite. "Hi," he said, like butter wouldn't melt in his mouth.

They couldn't see what had just happened—the destruction or the fear. The chaos he left behind in the air we were still breathing.

He went with them easily, like it was a sleepover. It was only meant to be a night or two.

But when given space and time to reflect, I gained realization and heartache over the situation and what I had to do.

It broke me, not because I gave up, but because I had held on so long—too long—believing nurture would outweigh nature in silence and shame.

Also, because letting him go, even after all the damage, still felt like a kind of grief and failure.

I handed Stephanie a letter of guardianship with a pen that felt heavier than it should have. It wasn't just ink—it was everything: my love, my grief, my final thread of hope. She wasn't just a friend anymore; she became the line between survival and catastrophe.

Jason needed help, and I couldn't give it anymore—not without risking the rest of us. Not without losing myself.

Every night I lay awake wondering if I'd done the right thing. My heart ached with guilt, but my body buzzed with terror at the thought of him returning. If I let him back into our home, we would not survive it. Something in me knew that with certainty—it wouldn't be just bruising next time, it would be worse.

So, I went to the police—not to press charges; I didn't want my son criminalized—but for guidance, support, something, a direction. I kept calling Child Protection every day for two weeks straight, desperate for someone to tell me I wasn't alone, desperate for someone to help me.

Instead, the system turned on me.

The police filed for an IVO—Jason the perpetrator—something I never requested. I only found out when they served the papers to me. It felt like a betrayal wrapped in legal ink, another decision made about me, not with me.

Then Child Protection called—but not with support, not with a plan. They came to investigate me. It had been three weeks now.

Because I wanted to relinquish care.

They stormed into my home like I was the danger—not Jason, me. They asked questions, sharp and loaded, then twisted my words like they'd already written the ending. They didn't hear my fear; they didn't see my injuries. They saw only a mother who wanted out, and they made that mean I was unfit, cold, and dangerous.

"If you relinquish one child, you relinquish them all," they said, like it was a policy, not a punishment. They didn't want to understand; they just wanted to control the narrative.

Just like that, before darkness had fully settled over the sky, they hit me with an order.

All three children. Removed. Effective immediately.

I begged, "If I leave, can Stephanie care for them?" I asked, sobbing, shaking. They said yes.

I kissed my children goodbye. I walked out of my own home, a mother with nothing in her arms but air and heartbreak.

The next day was a blur of waiting, legal deadlines, panic, and silence. Finally, Jennifer and Mark were returned to me. The order was adjusted; they were allowed to come home.

But Jason... Jason was to be transitioned back. I wanted to scream, to rip up the paperwork.

To tear the courtroom apart brick by brick, to have my voice heard.

Every cell in my body told me it wasn't safe, but they didn't care about gut instinct.

They only cared about their version of "fair."

I read the reports—the files, the judgments, the opinions of people who'd never stepped foot in our living room, never seen the bruises, never heard the midnight screams.

They wrote about me like I was the monster, like I had failed him.

Like all of this violence came from a mother who didn't love enough.

They didn't know the nights I held him in a hug and begged him to stay.

The dinners we cooked together, the jokes I tried to make, the softness I gave until it shattered me.

They didn't know I was already in therapy, that I was seeing a psychologist for my anxiety. That I was enrolled in parenting courses trying to understand teenagers. That I was trying— always trying—to help Jason express himself and heal his trauma.

Then came the final slap in the face. A worker asked me about a fight that happened at Karen's house—a fistfight between Jason and Karen, a violent incident that shook their walls. I didn't know anything about it; I wasn't there. But the moment I said that, the topic vanished—never raised again, never documented, never followed up.

Violence happened there, but it wasn't investigated. Instead, they'd already decided who the villain was—me—and that's when the deepest kind of heartbreak set in.

Not just the loss of a child, not just the trauma of abuse, but the soul-breaking weight of being painted as the problem when you were the only one screaming for help the whole time.

The Child Protection investigation dragged on for six long, silent months.

No check-ins, no contact, just silence. Right before the protective order was due to lapse, they filed for an extension—not because of a safety concern, but because they hadn't completed their paperwork. Their failure, their delay, but still... their control.

I didn't understand how the system worked; I still don't. I only knew that they held the power, and I didn't.

Jason remained in Stephanie's care, but everything started to unravel. Stephanie heard from Child Protection that she was "not suitable" as a guardian, and suddenly everything turned. The bond we had, the trust—it vanished. Out of hurt or fear or something darker, Stephanie began lying. She and Jason crafted a story together, and I watched helplessly as the system latched onto it without question.

It felt like retaliation—and it was. After all I'd endured, after the bruises, the sleepless nights, the violent outbursts, the endless begging for help.

Child Protection closed and withdrew the extension order. What I got was a letter.

A letter: "Thank you for your cooperation. Sorry for the inconvenience. Your file is now closed. Good luck." Good luck? What do you say to that? What do you say to a system that walks away without a word of acknowledgment, without seeing the damage they caused to someone who only ever tried to love?

I did love—so hard, so completely, with everything I had. Now I was left with a broken heart and a hole where my hope used to live.

I questioned every single moment of parenting—every word, every decision. Every time I said yes or no or held my breath or held my child.

No one called Child Protection when I was the child being abused. No one came for me, no one saved me, and still, I grew up and did everything I could not to be her. I tried to become the mother I never had—to be the best parent I could be—and even then, I still ended up the villain in someone else's story.

It shredded something inside me—all the hope, all the belief that I made a difference. All the comfort, guidance, and safety I thought I had built for my kids.

But slowly, quietly, Jennifer and Mark began to move more freely. There was a lightness returning to them that I hadn't seen in years. They started laughing again—real laughter, loud, silly, beautiful laughter. It was like air returning to lungs that had been holding their breath for too long.

Mark still hid when he saw Jason at school—the trauma doesn't vanish just because the threat does. But he moves easier now, he smiles more. Jennifer's spark is returning, the light that Jason's pain kept dimming.

I knew I had relationship repair work to do, so I called a family meeting.

I sat Jennifer and Mark down and told them the truth—gently, openly, fully. I told them I was sorry, that I hadn't always gotten it right. That sometimes, I had to make choices I didn't want to make—like pushing them aside to protect them. I told them Jason had to be number one because it was the only way to stop him from hurting them. I told them I was tired, and sad, and trying.

I told them I loved them, and then I listened. Together, we began rebuilding. I explained how we would begin family counselling, and they were welcome to have private sessions too.

We're not the same family we were—it's three from five, then four—but maybe that's okay. Because the sound of Jennifer and Mark laughing together, freely, joyfully, is the sound of survival. It's the sound of healing.

For the first time in a long time, I believe we're going to be okay.

Reflection: - lived experience of Grief

Grief is not limited to death. It shows up in many forms of loss: the end of a friendship, family connections breaking, losing a job, the loss of ability, or the painful disconnection from people or places that once gave us meaning. Every form of grief carries weight, and every loss matters.

All grief brings with it emotions that can feel overwhelming, unpredictable, or exhausting. Some losses may feel harder to carry than others, but every grief deserves space and acknowledgment. There is no right or wrong way to grieve, and there is no timeline. Some days feel easier, while other days a small reminder—a smell, a song, a place—can bring the weight of grief crashing back in.

Grief is not a straight line. It changes, shifts, and evolves. Sometimes it feels like heavy fog; other times it softens to a quiet ache. What doesn't change is that grief is a reflection of love. The deeper the love or the meaning, the more profound the grief.

Personal Reflection on Grief

Grief has followed me through many chapters of life, not just in death but in the quiet, hidden losses too—friendships that ended, family ties that broke, jobs I had to walk away from, abilities I no longer had, and the deep ache of lost connection. Each one carried its own weight. Some were sharp and unbearable, others were slow and hollow, but all of them left their mark.

I learnt that grief doesn't follow rules. It doesn't stay neat or predictable. Some days it feels softer, almost manageable, and then out of nowhere, a smell, a song, or a memory crashes in, and I am right back in the raw ache of loss. What once felt like weakness I now see as love; grief is a sign of how deeply something or someone mattered.

I used to believe I had to hide it—to keep strong and move on—but I know now that all feelings are okay. Sadness, anger, emptiness, even joy in the middle of it all—they all belong. There's no finish line, no "getting over it." Grief shifts, changes, and becomes part of you, but it doesn't mean life can't hold beauty again.

What gives me strength now is self-compassion. I remind myself that grief is not a failure to heal; it is healing in motion. It's messy, it's human, and it's proof that I have loved and lived.

Hope and Empowerment

Through grief, I have discovered something powerful: I can survive what I once thought I could not. Even in the darkest days, there were glimmers—a kind word, a shared story, a sunrise that reminded me I was still here.

Grief doesn't erase joy forever. It teaches me that moments of happiness and love can exist alongside pain. I don't need to choose one or the other—both can belong. Slowly, I am learning that grief is not just an ending but also an opening—a way to honour what was while making space for what can still be.

I am not broken by loss. I am reshaped by it. And within that reshaping, I find resilience, compassion, and strength I never knew I had. Grief will always walk beside me, but so will hope. That hope whispers: you are still here, and life can still hold meaning, beauty, and love.

Supporting Someone Through Grief

Do's and Don'ts

 DO

- **Listen with compassion**, sometimes silence and presence are more powerful than words.

- **Validate their feelings**, Remind them:
    - "Your grief is real."
    - "There is no wrong way to feel."
    - "It makes sense that you're hurting, it shows how much this mattered."

- **Respect their pace**, Healing cannot be rushed. Grief has no deadline.

- **Offer practical support**, bring a meal, run errands, help with childcare, or simply sit with them.

- **Check in regularly**, not just at the start. Grief can feel loneliest months later, when the world has moved on.

- **Acknowledge the loss**, speak their loved one's name or honour what was lost. Silence can feel like erasure.

- **Encourage gentle care**, Support small acts of rest, nourishment, and moments of joy.

✖ DON'T

- Don't say "You'll get over it" or "Time heals all wounds." These minimise pain.

- Don't avoid the person out of discomfort. Grief already feels isolating.

- Don't pressure them to "move on" or return to normal too quickly.

- Don't compare griefs, every loss is unique.

- Don't try to fix it. Your role is to walk beside them, not erase their pain.

- Don't disappear if they seem "okay." Grief often lingers long after it's visible.

Key Takeaway

Grief is not weakness; it is love in another form. It may never disappear, but it can transform. With compassion, patience, and support, it is possible to carry grief and still create a life filled with meaning, joy, and connection.

Chapter 13: Shattered Where I Should Have Been Safe

Poem: The Silence After the Storm

I let him in

because I thought I was safe,

because I still believed

that kindness could come

without a cost.

I froze

as my body betrayed me again,

paralysed in a room

I once called mine

now a crime scene

where the air forgot how to breathe.

I spoke.

For once, I told the truth

and the world closed its ears.

The police dragged their feet.

Justice took a nap.

And I was the one locked away

for wanting the pain to stop.

Karen crept in through the cracks,

wrapped her voice around mine

until I couldn't tell

where she ended

and I began.

Her hands weren't fists

but they held me down

just the same.

Jobs vanished like hope.

Every time I stood up,

someone cut the legs from beneath me.

Told me I was too much.

Too broken.

Too loud.

Too honest.

I became a shadow

of the woman I was trying to be

hollow-eyed,

empty-chested,

numb-fingered

from gripping onto nothing.

I wanted to disappear

not because I didn't want to live,

but because

no one made it safe

for me to stay.

"It wasn't just one act that broke me, it was everything that followed when I dared to speak."

Some chapters are written with trembling hands, eyes blurred by tears you thought had long dried. This is one of those chapters.

His name was Adam.

It began like so many other moments in my life, in the gray space between loneliness and longing. A local Facebook group called *Fun, Social and Outings* offered what I craved: adult conversation, company, and a glimpse of a world outside parenting, trauma, and surviving. It wasn't meant to be romantic or sexual, just a group of people finding connection through chats, meetups, camping trips. A friend of mine, Emma, had vouched for it; she made it sound safe, so I trusted it.

At first, I kept things light by comments on threads, nothing personal. It didn't take long for a private message to appear in Messenger; it was from Adam. We started talking through Messenger, just friendly chat that then led to voice calls, sometimes for hours.

He told me he was a solo dad to an older teen son. I shared things about Jason and the struggles I faced parenting a difficult child; he gave advice. At the time it felt genuine; now I question if maybe he knew exactly what to say to sound like he understood, and in fact he didn't care, he was just grooming.

I accepted his friend request and added him on Facebook. The conversations became a routine, something familiar to fall into when the house fell quiet. A kind of hidden life I was building, not out of shame, but because it was mine, separate from just being a boring old parent, just a mum.

Then I went to the Dunlara Show with my kid, a fun family day, sacred time for bonding and play. Adam was there; I didn't know it was him until he walked up to me, called my name, and introduced himself.

Adam told me he'd been following me around the show; my stomach dropped, my skin prickled. This wasn't a casual encounter, this was stalking. I froze, but then protection rose for my kids, and I acted in defense. "I'm with my kids," I snapped, trying to create distance. "This isn't the time." I turned my back and walked away.

It was jarring. He lived over an hour away. How did he know I'd be there? How did he recognize me? And why did he follow me?

I messaged Emma afterward, voice tight with unease. I needed someone to tell me I wasn't being paranoid. She said he was safe, that I was overthinking it. So I took on board her words of reassurance and silenced my instincts again.

Not long after, I posted an innocent update about an 8 km walk I'd done, feeling proud. I had blurred the street names on the map, but he pieced it together. Adam used landmarks, the terrain, maybe even subtle patterns I hadn't thought to hide, and figured out where I lived.

I felt sick, violated, and scared. I reached out to Emma, and again she reassured me Adam was harmless. I didn't want to be that woman who panics at every shadow, so I swallowed the discomfort and kept talking.

We agreed to meet in person, two friends just hanging out for coffee in Clydesford. The morning tea was fine—normal, adult conversation, no flirting, no touching. Just two people filling the gaps in their lives with some company; I missed that more than I could admit.

Weeks later we agreed to catch up. I took Jennifer, as she was always with me. We went bowling; it felt like the kind of grown-up day out I hadn't had in years. Fun, laughter, general chit-chat, and healthy competition.

But out of the blue, things shifted; that's when things started to turn. He sat too close, invaded my personal space, and his hands started to wander. He put a hand on my shoulder, touched the side of my leg like it was an accident—it wasn't completely inappropriate, but deliberate and calculated. I told myself I was too sensitive, that my radar was wrong, that my personal space and boundaries were disproportionate to everyone else's. I ignored the discomfort.

Then in the car park as we said goodbye, he reached down and touched me, over my clothes but directly over my vagina. It was brief, quick, and detonated something inside me; my whole body froze. I couldn't find my voice, couldn't react, but had to get away. I slipped swiftly into my car, closed the door, said nothing, just drove home in stunned silence.

That night Adam messaged, apologized, said he was just trying to help me "push past my comfort zone." I responded firmly: never touch me again, we are friends, I do not want any relationships!

Somehow that was enough for me to stay, retain our friendship. I told myself boundaries had been set, that Adam now understood and would respect them. I still needed the friendship, the adult connection, the soothing rhythm of routine, so I allowed the problem to be sorted and retained the friendship.

Then came the night that broke me.

Adam called; he mentioned he was upset, told me stories around family stuff, he sounded low and vulnerable. I'd learnt to offer comfort because I so often needed it myself. Adam had been my sounding board before and after Jason left. It was just me, Jennifer, and her friend Samantha at home. Mark was at Nana's. The house was quiet; I was emotionally exhausted—the kind of tired that makes you second-guess yourself.

Adam asked if he could come over. I said no, not once or twice but repeatedly. I told him I wasn't interested and it was late; I wasn't his girlfriend and I wasn't a late-night hookup. But the calls kept coming, the messages, and the guilt trips—the story of a man driving around in distress, with the twist he was already in town, parked nearby now.

I should have said no, but I didn't. I was worn down. I felt responsible for his well-being. I told him he could come for a coffee and clearly stated, "You cannot stay. You cannot sleep here. You will have to drive home."

He arrived, slouched and quiet, looked sad and exhausted. I boiled the kettle and made the drinks, and he sat beside me on the couch. Adam told me I looked tired. I said I had a headache, and he said he could help, offering a massage.

I said yes. My body was aching, head pounding, stress clinging to every muscle. Part of me just wanted to feel kindness, nonsexual touch—something healing and relaxing.

I led him to my room, fully clothed, lights on, door open. I trusted I would be safe, that the offer was for assistance, not evil and deceit. I lay down on my bed, flat on my stomach, trusting this moment to stay safe.

It wasn't.

It started slow, gentle, hands on my back above all my layers of clothing. A few minutes into it something shifted—the touch changed, became rough, invading, and intimate. His hands slid where they were never invited. My heart started pounding; my breath and words caught in my throat. I froze.

I froze, just like I used to when I was a child.

The room disappeared. I was no longer a woman; I was a little girl again, back in a body that never listened to me. A voice that refused to work. I wanted to scream; I wanted to fight, but nothing came out. I hated myself in that moment—not just for freezing, but for letting him in, for not seeing the red flags, for putting my daughter and her friend at risk, and for believing he was safe.

He was strong and determined. I said no. I whispered it, then repeated it over and over, louder. I tried to twist away, make it difficult, but he didn't care; he just kept going and completed what he wanted.

I lay there, silent, limbs limp, head filled like a whirlwind, my body betrayed me again. It always does—freezes—no matter how hard I try, I can't get that scream out, hit, kick, or push them to the side. When he was done, I rolled over, I pretended to sleep. He so kindly threw a blanket over me and left like nothing happened.

I waited until I heard the door close, the car start, and drive off. Then I leapt up, checked the kids, checked the house, and locked the doors. The girls' room door was exactly as I left it; Adam hadn't gone near them, thank God.

But the guilt devoured me. What if he had? What kind of mother lets someone like that in their house? What kind of woman lets herself be raped again?

I couldn't go back into my room. Just standing in the doorway it all replayed—the violation, what Adam did. I was never going to be the same.

I sat curled in the corner of the lounge room, shivering, skin crawling, every part of me screaming, how did this happen again?

The flashbacks came fast—of other nights, my sister, other men, other hands. My body remembered what I'd tried to forget. The childhood sexual abuse, the silence, the freezing, the shame, and now this—another violation in a lifetime of them.

But this time I was an adult. I was in control. I had made the poor choices, and the consequences were mine to hold… my poor choices with my daughter and friend sleeping down the hall. I let him in, the villain I brought risk into all.

I went to work the next day. I shouldn't have; my body was aching, my mind scattered, my insides hollowed out by the night before. But I went anyway, because pretending things were normal felt safer than sitting with the truth.

I moved through my shift like a ghost in my own skin. Everything looked the same, but nothing felt right. The memory of the night clung to me—on my clothes, in my hair, under my skin. Every noise startled me. Every smell brought me back to that room. I was silent, but inside I was screaming.

When my shift ended, I sat in my car, keys in hand, not knowing what to do. The world outside kept moving, but I was stuck, frozen again. I picked up my phone and called a friend, someone I trusted. I asked for her advice, hesitant and ashamed. She didn't hesitate. "You need to go to the police," she said. "He needs to be stopped."

Her words cut through the fog; something shifted inside me.

For years, I'd carried the guilt of never reporting my father, never protecting my sister, never speaking the truth about the old man. I'd lived with the consequences of silence—not just mine, but others'. The ache of knowing someone else might get hurt because I didn't speak.

This time, I was an adult. This time, I had a chance to do what no one ever did for me. This time, I would choose accountability, even if it terrified me, even if it broke me.

With shaking hands and a voice so small it barely registered, I called the local police station.

"I need to report a sexual assault," I said, barely above a whisper. They told me someone would call me back.

It wasn't long before the phone rang—an officer's voice on the line, clear, calm, professional. The police said they needed to come to the house immediately. Evidence needed to be collected—items, clothing, DNA, camera footage, and a full statement. He was kind, but the urgency in his voice made everything real.

I looked around my house. Jennifer was home. There was no way I could have this conversation with her in earshot, no way I could cry, crumble, or speak about what happened with her nearby.

I tried calling friends—anyone who might be able to take her— but no one was free. No one answered. One by one, the options fell away.

I was desperate, so I called Karen. I begged. I told her I needed her to take Jennifer now.

She refused unless I explained why, so I felt obliged and told her. I told her what happened, what I was about to do, and why it mattered. Instead of support, I was met with cruelty.

Her voice came through the phone sharp and venomous:

"You can sure pick 'em." "Why the hell did you let him in?" "You always have to have someone, don't you?" "You deserved this." "It's all your fault."

Each word landed like a blow to the chest. Like I always had, I absorbed it, stored it, built it into the core belief system I've carried since childhood: I'm the problem. I deserve this. I should have known better.

She came and took Jennifer—not with compassion, but with disgust. I stood there, silently swallowing every insult, every judgment, because I had no fight left in me. I just needed my daughter to be safe. That was all that mattered now.

The police arrived soon after. My heart sank when I recognized one of the officers—she ran the local Little Aths club. She knew me, my kids, my community. The shame deepened. I felt exposed, like the walls around my private pain had been ripped away.

I walked them through the house, through the events of that night. Pointed to the couch, the bedroom, the door. They collected evidence, packaged up clothing, gathered anything they could. I stood to the side, trembling and sobbing uncontrollably.

The guilt poured out of me in waves. How didn't I see it coming? Why did I ignore the red flags? How did I put my daughter at risk like that?

It felt like drowning in a memory I couldn't escape—the shame of being raped in my own home again, just like the shame of being abused as a child, of staying silent then, and hating myself for it ever since.

I thought I had healed. I thought surviving Jason's violence had strengthened me.

I thought I'd made it through the worst of it.

But this dropped me into a darker pit than I had ever known— a place so heavy, so consuming, I didn't even know how to scream from it.

As the police finished up, they connected me with CASA (Centre Against Sexual Assault). They handed me the phone. I tried to speak, but nothing coherent came out. I was a shell— tears streaming, throat tight, words trapped beneath fear and grief and disbelief.

How do you explain the way a single night can collapse everything you thought you were rebuilding? How do you explain the ache of being hurt in the same way again after you worked so hard to believe you were finally safe?

I didn't sleep that night. I barely breathed. I had to go back to the station for the formal statement, the full taped interview, the legal process. The report had been made; it was official now and documented.

I had done it, but I was petrified. Every sound outside made me jump. Every creak in the floorboards felt like him returning. Every moment alone in that house felt like a new invasion.

I was terrified he would come back, terrified he'd hurt me for speaking up, terrified of how much more of myself I'd have to lose before anyone actually believed I didn't deserve this.

The investigation didn't feel like justice. It felt like another kind of violation. It was slow, messy, disjointed, full of promises with no weight behind them—endless phone calls, trips to the station, retelling my story over and over again while the man who raped me walked freely, untouched, unbothered.

The first time I returned to the police station for my formal interview, they asked me to do something I wasn't prepared for. They wanted me to call Adam; they wanted me to try and get him to confess on tape.

I was still in shock, still traumatized, still holding the shame and guilt like it was mine to carry. They wanted me to play a role, like this was some undercover sting operation. They handed me a phone and a script I couldn't emotionally stomach.

What they didn't know—or maybe didn't care to ask—was that in my rage and desperation, I had already tried to expose him. I had posted publicly on his Facebook wall, unable to hold the silence any longer: "Who will you sexually abuse and ignore next?"

Yes, it was impulsive. Yes, it compromised the investigation. But I had been silenced my entire life—as a child, as a teen, as a mother—and for once I needed to scream the truth, even if only in pixels. I needed his friends to see, people to hear the truth. I needed him to know I wasn't going to be quiet this time. But that post cost me.

At the station, when I dialled his number, he didn't answer. He ignored each and every attempt I made. He had already moved on—no apology, no remorse, not even the courtesy of pretending to be human.

Later, I received a text from him—not about the assault, not about my pain—but to say he had to go to Queensland because he felt like he had cheated on a former girlfriend. That was it. That was his explanation, as if what happened between us had been consensual, as if I had invited it.

I showed the texts to the officers, and they handed me a device—a recording unit—and told me to keep trying, keep calling, keep playing the part.

I left that station in tears. There was no protection, no IVO, no supervision, no clear plan—just a trauma survivor expected to chase down her own abuser for proof.

Each phone call was like reopening a wound. I hated myself for dialling, hated myself for pretending. Each unanswered ring felt like another silence I couldn't escape. Eventually, I returned the device—no confession, no progress, just more shame.

They said they'd try to go see him, but it was hard to organize and time-consuming as he was living over an hour away. They weren't sure when it would happen. Then he went to Queensland, and everything stalled again.

I felt exposed, unprotected, dismissed. I couldn't live like that.

The silence was too loud, and the trauma was too heavy. The police had done nothing. Karen was back in my home, pushing herself into my life again with the same old manipulation and emotional violence. I was drowning in pain, guilt, flashbacks, and the growing terror that I had once again let someone hurt me—and maybe he would hurt others.

I believed with every part of my damaged heart that this was my fault. If I disappeared, the danger would stop.

I wrote letters to my children, quietly, methodically, like I was packing up pieces of my soul to leave behind. Not because I didn't love them, but because I did. The truth of my headspace told me they deserved better than the broken mother I had become.

I got in my car and left, intending never to return. I planned to vanish—to kill myself where no one would find me. I didn't feel like a person anymore; I felt like evidence, like waste, like danger to those around me.

But someone noticed, and I was found, talked down, stopped in my tracks, ending all my plans. I didn't get to act, but I desperately wanted that moment to have an ending of peace.

In the aftermath, I wasn't given trauma-informed care, safety, or even kindness. I was institutionalized, locked away in a mental health facility for my own protection, as if I was the one who needed punishment. The man who raped me was entitled to freedom, and I was the problem for speaking.

I was drowning, and they gave me more weight. How could this be justice? I sat in that place day after day, surrounded by locked doors and routine, while Adam lived his life untouched, unchecked, unbothered.

Four months passed, then finally they interviewed him. They took his weapons, issued an interim intervention order. Four months after the rape! Four months of torture and silence! Four months where I thought my life meant nothing.

Still, Adam fought it. He contested the IVO. Not to clear his name, not to own what he did, but because he wanted his guns and phone back. That was what mattered to him—his power, his pride, his property. Not the woman he violated, not the life he shattered.

The months bled into years—delays, excuses, paperwork, pain. The final blow came fourteen months after I reported the rape—the case was dropped. Not because the evidence wasn't there, not because he was cleared, but because I was considered too mentally unstable to testify, because I had tried to end my life, because I had been institutionalized for surviving what he did to me. They decided it wasn't "in my best interest" to prosecute.

Just like that, it was over—no court, no trial, no justice. I was the one who had been raped, but I was treated as the liability. I was seen as the risk once again; I was the villain in a story where I had only ever tried to survive.

How do you process that? How do you walk through the world after that, knowing that the system meant to protect you chose silence over truth, abandonment over justice? I still don't understand it. I still can't make peace with it. I still don't know how to forgive myself for believing, even for a moment, that things could be different.

While the police investigation dragged on—fractured, slow, and endlessly retraumatizing—another kind of violence was unfolding quietly inside my own home.

Karen—she wasn't loud; she didn't need to be. Her weapons weren't fists but words, glances, silences. Lies delivered in a soothing voice, wrapped in twisted versions of love and concern. While the world saw her as the helper, the ex who stepped in when I needed support, the truth is Karen was another kind of abuser—just harder to name.

She moved back in like a shadow, seamlessly, as if she had a right to be there. I let her, not because I wanted her, but because I was too exhausted to resist. I was broken, traumatized, and desperate for something that resembled safety. Karen saw that, and she used it.

She took full advantage of my vulnerable state, just like she always had. Except this time, I was too numb to fight it, too stripped of belief in myself. The rape had already robbed me of trust, voice, and clarity. Karen simply walked in and claimed what was left.

At first, it was subtle. She offered help, managed things around the house, said she was doing it for me. Little by little, she chipped away at my independence until there was none left. Her control was suffocating and total.

She took over my phone, watched who I messaged, checked what I said. I was no longer allowed to talk freely to friends. If they came over, she would glare, make snide remarks, or be outright rude until they left and never came back.

Eventually, they stopped coming altogether. The isolation wasn't accidental—it was designed. Because when I had no one else, I only had her.

When I tried to speak up for myself, I was told I was overreacting, selfish, damaged. "You always ruin things," she'd say. "You're a drama queen. You're not well." Over and over again until I started saying those things to myself.

The insults were dressed up as "jokes." Constant little stabs at my parenting, my body, my mind, my choices. I was too emotional, too sensitive, too much of a mess. "You're lucky I'm still here," she'd remind me. "No one else would put up with you." And I believed her.

She crushed my sense of worth so thoroughly that I forgot what it felt like to believe I was good. I stopped trusting my instincts; I second-guessed every thought. My guilt, my shame, my desperation—all of it was filtered through her voice, her judgments, her reality.

I wasn't allowed to disagree with her—not without consequences. Silent treatment, sulking, gaslighting. "You said that, not me." "You're making things up again." "You only hear what you want to hear." It didn't take long before I stopped trying to explain myself.

Her voice became my voice; I spoke her words sometimes without realizing it. I repeated her opinions, saw myself through her lens. She rewrote my beliefs, my truth, my story. I wasn't a woman anymore; I wasn't even a person. I was a reflection of her projections—shaped, twisted, and controlled.

She made me feel like I was failing as a mother, that I was damaging my kids by simply existing. She turned my pain into proof that I was inadequate. "You can't even protect them," she'd whisper, or imply with a look. "They're better off when I'm in charge."

I believed I was unlovable. I believed I was dangerous. I believed I was no one, and that without her, I would disappear.

Beneath all that pain, something quietly resisted—a part of me, small, quiet, almost dead, began to notice what was happening. Two people helped bring that flicker of truth back to life: my therapist and a support worker from a local well-being service.

They never told me to leave; they never pushed. They just listened. Week after week, they heard what I couldn't say. They noticed the patterns, the tension, the silences, the borrowed language. They saw that I was being slowly erased.

They planted a seed—a gentle, quiet, consistent truth: this isn't love. This is control. This is abuse. At first, I resisted; I defended Karen. I couldn't hold the idea that she, too, was harming me—especially when I was already so destroyed by someone else. It felt like betrayal; it felt impossible, but they kept holding space, naming what I couldn't, and eventually, I walked into The Orange Door.

I didn't walk in calling it domestic violence—not yet. I didn't have the language. I just knew I couldn't keep living like this. I told them it was "complicated," "difficult," "toxic." But deep down, I was beginning to understand I needed her to leave, or I wouldn't survive.

It wasn't easy. Karen had stolen my voice, rewritten my mind, controlled my life. Saying no felt like jumping off a cliff. I feared how she'd react, scared of the silence that would follow, scared I wouldn't know who I was without her.

But over time, I built the courage. With the support of my therapist and the well-being worker, I took it one step at a time. I made small decisions, spoke a little louder, asked for help. Eventually, slowly, bravely, trembling, I asked Karen to leave.

She didn't go easily, but she went. And for the first time in a long time, the house was quiet. Not just silent—quiet, peaceful, still. In that stillness, I began to find pieces of myself again—tiny pieces, real, untouched, mine.

Among all of this—the rape, the investigation, the mental health system, Karen's manipulation—I lost something else: faith.

Faith in my ability to function, to contribute, to be useful. Faith that I was even capable of surviving life in the real world anymore. Every time I tried to hold on, the ground shifted beneath me, and something was ripped away.

Work had always been an anchor for me—a space where I could flip my cap, smile at customers, focus on a task, and forget. Forget the trauma, the chaos, the pain. In the simplest sense, work meant purpose—it meant I was still someone.

But even that was taken. At the time, I was working closing shifts at a local servo. I wasn't coping—not with nights, not with responsibility, not with the growing anxiety that clawed through me the second the sun dipped below the horizon.

I gathered every ounce of courage I had and went to my boss. I told them the truth. I told them I'd been raped. I told them I wasn't coping with being alone at night, that supervising junior staff while managing flashbacks and crippling fear wasn't safe for me or anyone else.

I didn't ask for pity; I asked for different shifts—something lighter, something manageable. Their response? "If you can't do the job you were hired for, then you need to move on." Just like that—no support, no conversation, no human compassion. I was dismissed on the spot.

Speaking the truth again had become the reason I was punished. I walked out of that job with tears in my eyes and shame clawing at my throat. Why do I even try? I thought. Why does telling the truth always come with a cost I can't afford?

For four months, I spiraled. Unemployed, alone, ashamed. Eventually, I tried again at a different servo. New faces, new chance, and at first, I was thriving. I loved that job; I loved the distraction, the rhythm, the pride of doing something well. But the court reminders, the legal delays, the rape case that was still dragging out in the background—they didn't disappear just because I wore a uniform.

Sometimes, when the numbness got too much, I turned on myself. One night, in the thick of it, I punched my hand hard to feel something, anything. I hit it until it broke. The pain was real; it was proof I was still alive.

I didn't lie about it. I told my boss the truth: I need a week just to breathe, to reset, to gather myself. To his credit, he agreed, but when I tried to return, medical clearance in hand, my cast wrapped around the reminder of pain, the tone shifted. He said I was a liability, that I couldn't return until the cast was off and I was fully recovered.

I still held onto hope, still believed I had a job to go back to. Weeks later, cast off, another doctor's note in hand, I returned. They called a meeting, and once again, I was dismissed.

Told I was too much trouble, too much risk, too unpredictable. I sat there, stunned, dazed. I had done nothing wrong on the job. I showed up, I worked hard, I left my baggage at the door, but it didn't matter. The truth—my truth—had made me disposable again.

I left that meeting in silence. I walked to the shops, bought supplies, and planned another suicide attempt, because how much rejection can one person take?

How many times can you be told, with words or silence, that you're a burden, a liability, an inconvenience?

I didn't feel like a person anymore; I felt like a walking warning label. A problem too complex to deal with. I wasn't just unemployed; I was unworthy.

But the universe, in all its strange mercy, gave me one more rope to hold onto. About seven months later, I saw an ad for a local op shop. An old friend, Olivia, was running it. I reached out. Told her everything. As I cried, she listened. She didn't flinch; she didn't turn away. She said, "Come in. Volunteer. Let's just start there." So, I did, and I loved it.

I found purpose again—connection, laughter, belonging. I showed up every day, took pride in every shelf I stocked, every customer I helped. I worked with Olivia like we'd been doing it for years. After three months, she offered me a paid role as Assistant Manager.

I couldn't believe it; I didn't think I stood a chance. Olivia saw something in me I'd forgotten existed. Slowly, I began to believe I was capable again. Two days a week, I ran the shop solo—confident, calm, competent.

Then came the storm—not caused by me, but around me. Workplace bullying from higher up, internal politics—nothing to do with me. Olivia, the only person who had stood up for me, who had believed in me, stood her ground. She refused to let it happen.

So she left. Olivia walked out, and in her leaving, the floor crumbled beneath me. I couldn't stay without her. The thought of starting over again, without support, without someone who understood—I couldn't do it. I locked up the shop, dropped the key at the police station, and I left.

Another suicide attempt, because once again, I had lost the one place where I felt human. The one place where my pain didn't make me a problem. Olivia found me again. She saved my life. I will be forever grateful.

Since then, I haven't worked. I sit on a disability pension, swallowed by fear. Afraid that if I try again, my mental health will be judged. That I'll be deemed unstable, unfit. That my pain will once again be used as evidence that I'm not enough. I carry the shame of believing I'm a burden. I live with the belief that I am unemployable. That I ruin everything. That I am a liability, not a person. That I will always mess it up, even when I don't—and I don't know how to undo that story.

It's been written into me by every employer who walked away. Every support person who turned their back. Every system that saw my honesty as a threat instead of a cry for help.

Maybe, just maybe, writing this is the start of rewriting that story. Maybe survival itself means I haven't ruined everything.

The rape was the beginning of the end of me.

It cracked something deep inside—not just my sense of safety, but my belief that I could survive this life anymore. From that night forward, I wasn't living. I was barely existing. I carried shame like skin, guilt like oxygen.

Karen's return, her coercive control, her manipulation, her slow erosion of myself didn't stop when she left the house. Her voice still echoed in my head, wrapped around my thoughts, shaping my beliefs. She had stolen my voice so many times that even in her absence, I couldn't hear myself anymore.

Then came the job losses, one after the other. Each time I tried to speak my truth, I was met with silence, judgment, or punishment. I wasn't seen as brave; I was seen as unstable. Each rejection confirmed what I already feared—that I was unworthy, unfixable, and unwanted. I was left in a place of total despair. No direction, no connection, no hope.

I turned on myself. Self-harm became my only release. Suicide, my only way out. Each attempt wasn't about wanting to die—it was about needing the pain to stop. Needing someone to see me, to hear me. To believe that I wasn't the problem—I was the product of a thousand unspeakable things. I didn't know how to keep going, so I stopped trying.

Chapter 14: The Pain Beneath the Skin

Poem: "Beneath the Skin"

I wore my pain beneath the skin,

No bruises bright enough to win

A glance, a hand, a whispered care

Just silence thick within the air.

A bandage here, a bruised-up knee,

A quiet, aching, hidden plea.

I wanted someone, anyone,

To see the hurt I could not run.

They didn't see so I withdrew,

My world went quiet, cold, and blue.

When I screamed, it made no sound,

Just thudding fists against the ground.

I broke my bones to break the ache,

To prove the sadness wasn't fake.

I bled in silence, burnt in shame,

Each scar a chapter, never named.

I spiralled slow, I planned, I fell,

But didn't want to say farewell.

I didn't want to end my life

I just needed the internal pain to stop.

Some called me selfish, cold, unwell,

Dismissed me with a patient's shell.

But I was human, lost, afraid

And tired of the price I'd paid.

Then one day, a handheld mine

No lecture, pity, or deadline.

Just presence soft enough to stay,

And hold the storm until it lay.

I still hear whispers in my mind,

But now, I search, and sometimes find

A cup of tea, a daughter's hug,

A friend who sits upon the rug.

Not every pain can be undone,

But in the dark, I've seen the sun.

And though the night still calls my name,

I'm learning how to stay.

To hold on tight and ride the waves to stay.

"Some wounds don't bleed. Some deaths don't end a life. And sometimes, surviving is the most violent act of all."

I used to think my journey with self-harm and suicidality began after Adam raped me. That trauma tore through everything I thought I knew about safety and self-worth. But while writing this memoir, I began to see clearly: the signs were there long before.

My self-harm started quietly, invisibly, and much earlier, in childhood. I remember jamming my fingers in doors, hitting my hand on hard surfaces. Nothing severe at first, just enough to feel something, or maybe it was to be seen. Sometimes I'd wrap a bandage around my wrist or my knee, pretending it was injured. At school, I'd wear it like a badge, hoping someone might notice, dig a little deeper, and see the pain and hidden truth that lay at the roots of it all. The kid with the broken arm was always surrounded, always asked about. I wasn't jealous of their injury; I was desperate for their attention, to be seen and heard.

I didn't have the language for it back then; I didn't know how to say, "I'm not okay." I couldn't find the words to describe the emptiness or the ache in my chest. I didn't know how to tell someone that I was dissociated, disconnected, and numb. So, I used pain, real or faked, as a way to express what I had no voice for. My injuries were on the inside, but I needed people to see something; I needed them to see the emotional pain from my family's abuse that was hurting me.

No one did, or if they did, they didn't speak to it. That silence confirmed the story I was already telling myself: I didn't matter.

Eventually, I stopped for a long time, decades even. But the pain never really left; it just got quieter, hidden beneath adult responsibilities and survival. Then, like all suppressed wounds, it returned, louder, sharper, and more frequently, with extreme intensity.

Self-harm made a sudden yet rapid comeback in adulthood. This time, I didn't want it to be seen; I went out of my way to hide it. I did it to feel; I needed to stop the emotional pain that was not a real, visible pain, and to let in and feel something that was real, and that real was physical pain to me.

The hitting returned, fists slammed into walls, feet into furniture. I'd bruise myself, sometimes even break bones. I didn't tell the truth when asked, instead I created stories to cover it up. "I fell," "I tripped"; the guilt and shame were unbearable. The fear of being found out, of being judged, all kept me silent.

It wasn't about attention anymore; it was about an emotional release, about control. About needing to translate unbearable emotional pain into something physical, something I could understand and manage. Bruises fade, broken bones heal, but what do you do with a soul that feels fractured?

Then came method 1: watching blood slowly trickle from my skin felt like releasing the chaos inside. It gave me a moment of calm, a sense of control.

Method 2 came after that, a more calculated pain. I controlled how long I held it; I decided when to stop. It gave me power in a world that so often stripped it away. But the burns would always get infected, no matter how carefully I treated them. Just like my internal wounds: hidden, inflamed, festering.

Self-harm was the lesser of the two evils when it came to my coping skills. If I used self-harm, I could get the release and de-escalate the emotional pain that I was experiencing, regain some control, and stop it from escalating to suicide attempts. Not healthy, I know, but to me it was harm minimization, and, in that moment, I was still in survival mode, so all these maladaptive strategies had their place and purpose. To help me keep living, to keep breathing, to keep going, one foot in front of the other, minute by minute, hour by hour.

My first contact as a bystander with someone who had attempted suicide was that of a close friend of mine. I am guilty of believing, at the time, she was selfish: why? how? Should have, could have. It wasn't until much later, when I experienced the intensity myself firsthand, that I felt an intense amount of guilt and shame that I held that same bias and view that most others had held.

Honestly, in the moment of my own experience, it was my children, my friends, and my family I was thinking about. I believed those lies my brain was telling me, that I was better off gone, that being around was a problem to those in my life. I learnt a valuable lesson here, that is, I believe that lived and living experience can only ever truly understand the process you are going through if you have been in the situation firsthand. This led me to be forgiving of those who couldn't understand me and my pain, or my thought process.

I used to think my journey with suicide began after Adam raped me. That was the first time I started writing notes, goodbye letters, the first time I planned to end my life. But when I look back honestly, I can see that suicidality lived in me long before. As a young teen, I would hold my breath until I blacked out, hoping that if I stopped breathing, I'd disappear. I didn't even call it suicide; I didn't understand it that way; it just felt like relief and an answer to escape the horrible place I was forced to live in.

I didn't truly understand how deeply I was hurting until I left home and began drinking. Alcohol lowered all my walls; with every drink, I lost my ability to mask and my filter; the suicidal urges grew louder. I begged people, sometimes strangers, for something lethal, not because I had a plan. Not because I wanted to die, but because I couldn't survive this anymore. I needed the nightmares to stop haunting me; the memories I had pushed so deep, and the truth I had avoided so hard, to stop chasing after me.

Suicidality wasn't sudden or constant; it came in waves. Some were small ripples, others were tidal, crashing over me when I least expected it. There was a strict pattern: get the kids safe, isolate myself, and make another attempt. It wasn't always about death; it was about ending the pain. It was about getting a break, and seeing no other way of achieving it, being so stuck, lonely, with no choice or options left to explore.

Most times followed a particular pattern, and that pattern was followed on autopilot. I wrote letters, cleaned the house, fed the pets, folded the washing. I planned, I prepared, then I attempted. Sometimes I would call for help, sometimes I was intercepted. I am fortunate to say I have had a 100% survival rate.

On multiple occasions, I walked into emergency departments asking for help. Mute, unable to speak, I handed over handwritten notes. The response could determine whether I lived or died. One nurse saw me approach and said loudly, "She's a VIP here. Very impatient, she'll probably leave." And I did, because if they couldn't support me or believe in me, why was I even willing to try?

I walked straight out... and straight into another attempt. When I came back in through an ambulance, everything changed. Then, suddenly, I was "a medical patient"; then, they treated me. Then, they saw me, but only after I nearly died.

Each interaction that dismissed me added another scar, internal, invisible, but agonizing. They weren't being cruel, I told myself. They were just doing their job; I'm not worthy; I'm not sick; I don't belong here. But the truth was, I felt punished for being unwell; I felt shamed for being honest, but, worst of all, I felt judged for asking for help.

Eventually, I stopped asking; instead, I lied, I masked it, I suffered silently. Because it felt safer—less judgment, less control, and less domination from professionals. Even Lifeline became unsafe; if I was too honest, they'd involve services. If

I wasn't honest enough, they'd hang up and dismiss me with brush-offs like take a shower, go for a walk, keep busy.

So, I spiraled every three to six weeks, alone, just trying to get through the best I could. I noticed it was often around my period. Hormones? Maybe. Trauma? Definitely. But I was too ashamed to talk about it anymore; my thoughts, my voice, diminished to nothing that anyone would hear or value as a form of input.

Living with constant suicidality, anxiety, and depression became the new norm for me. Suicidality wasn't a single crisis or a single event; it was a daily thought that changed in intensity. It was a process, a cycle that went around in a circle or up and down in waves.

It often starts with numbness, a void so deep, nothing can reach it. I shut down, I disconnect, I become mute. Then comes the emotional flooding—tears that don't stop, sadness that drowns me. Overwhelm at the smallest things, trying to function while feeling like I'm breaking apart.

Lastly, fear, the worst one of them all. Fear of myself, fear of what I might do to myself, fear of the pattern I can't escape. In those moments, I want to ask for help; I try to reach out. A text, a chat, a note, but I don't know what I'll get in return.

Will I be heard and helped, or dismissed and rejected? Will I be given help, or will I be punished with control and power? Will I be given choice, or stripped of my voice, judged and told what to do?

That fear alone has kept me from speaking, reaching out, taking away my potential to be living.

Through my journey, I found there to be three different approaches when I did reach out. Each approach had an impact on the choice I made. I know I'm accountable for my choices—I don't ever deny that—but I hope, in sharing the impact, that others can stop and see the difference the responses make in my actions.

One. I reached out to a helpline; they encouraged me to go to the emergency room. I arrived; they hung up. I was abandoned, and I was left alone. Those false voices spoke loudly in my head and told me I was worthless and not deserving. A nurse judged me loudly. I walked out and attempted suicide, again.

Two. I entered a peer space; someone sat with me. No judgment, no fixing, just presence. They walked with me to the hospital, stayed by my side, and handed me over gently. I stayed; I survived.

Three. It was midnight; I sent a desperate text to a friend. She drove through fog, a lengthy drive to sit with me, to hold me. She didn't talk, she didn't fix; she just placed her hand on my shoulder and sat beside my bed. That was enough; that saved me.

Here I would like to slip in a little bit of my story I share now in suicide prevention; it's about informing others, educating to have a better understanding.

Have you ever received a cryptic message? A message that made you pause, but you weren't sure what to do?

Have you ever heard someone say, "I wish I was dead"? Did you feel panic, or did you brush it off?

Would you recognize these signs?

- Someone becoming withdrawn
- Someone suddenly upbeat

- Someone making final arrangements

Do you realize your response could mean life or death? I live with suicidality; it's my reality.

I've survived multiple attempts. I stand here not just to tell my story, but to educate, to break silence, and save others.

Stigma isolates, judgment harms, silence kills.

Let me show you what it's like inside the mind of someone suicidal:

- "I'm not good enough."
- "I'm a burden."
- "I'm unlovable."
- "Everyone would be better off without me."

These aren't thoughts. They are truths in that moment. Suicidality is not logical; it's not linear. It's fear, it's pain, it's trauma.

You don't have to be a professional to make a difference!!!!! My 13-year-old daughter doesn't know the full story, but she sees me. When I'm struggling, she:

- Makes me tea
- Gives me a hug
- Places our cat beside me
- Holds my hand

No words, just presence, her love has saved me more times than she'll ever know.

If she can do that, so can you.

You don't have to fix it; you don't have to say the perfect thing. You just have to care enough to show up.

Because surviving the darkest moments is not something anyone can do alone.

If you live with suicidality: You are not broken, you are not beyond repair. You are human and you are not alone.

There is hope, even in the darkest hour, there is always hope.

Reflection: - Lived Experience of Depression, Anxiety, Self-Harm & Suicidality

Living with depression, anxiety, self-harm, and suicidal thoughts is not about weakness or failure; it is about survival under circumstances that can feel unbearable. Each of these experiences brings its own weight, its own kind of storm, yet they are often invisible to those around us.

Depression consumes the mind in a way that is almost impossible to explain. It isn't simply sadness or tiredness—it's a darkness that seeps into every thought, every breath, every corner of who I am. Rumination becomes a trap with no beginning or end, replaying mistakes, regrets, and self-criticism endlessly. On the outside, I might function—working, parenting, smiling—but inside, I'm trapped in a cage no one else can see.

Anxiety feels like carrying a storm inside me that never stops. It's a constant alarm, scanning for danger even when there is none. A simple phone call, walking into a shop, or sitting in a waiting room can feel like walking into a battlefield. Social situations feel like being under a spotlight—every word and action under intense scrutiny, leaving me drained and replaying moments long after they have passed. Anxiety is not overreacting; it is an internal struggle most people never witness.

Self-harm was my survival tool when nothing else could quiet the chaos. It wasn't about attention; it was about control, release, and survival. Every scar tells a story—not of weakness, but of managing unbearable emotions. What helped wasn't punishment or shame; it was presence, patience, and validation. Someone who could sit with me in the mess without turning away made all the difference. Slowly, I learnt safer ways to release my pain and to reconnect with life, piece by piece.

Suicidality is not always about wanting to die—it can be about wanting the pain to stop, wanting relief from the chaos inside. At times, it is quiet and seductive, whispering, "You can rest now." Other times, it is loud and suffocating. For years, I carried this in silence, afraid of being judged or misunderstood. Speaking it—even shakily, even to one trusted person—lessened the darkness and reminded me that connection matters.

Over time, I began to shift from surviving to living, from despair to small glimmers of hope. I discovered that healing doesn't mean these struggles disappear—it means I have learnt ways to live with them, to navigate the storms, and to reclaim my sense of self. Presence, compassion, and support became my lifelines. I learnt that needing help is human, asking for support is courage, and that my lived experience is not a burden—it is a strength.

I want anyone who reads this to know: you are not broken. Your coping mechanisms are not failures. Your pain is real, valid, and deserving of attention and care. Healing is possible, one small step at a time, with safe people, supportive practices, and compassion for yourself. There is hope, even in the darkest moments. You are not alone.

Hope, Resilience & Empowerment

Even in the darkest moments, hope can exist—often quietly, as a small flicker. It doesn't always feel grand or obvious, but it is enough to keep you moving forward, one breath, one step, one day at a time. Hope reminds us that the storm inside will not last forever, and that healing, even if slow, is possible.

Resilience is not about never feeling pain or never struggling; it is about surviving despite it. It is about rising again after being knocked down, even when the world feels heavy and unfair. Every day you continue, every moment you face your fears, every time you reach out for support, you are proving your strength. You are resilient, even when you doubt it.

Empowerment comes from reclaiming control over your own story. It is the courage to speak your truth, to set boundaries, to care for yourself, and to make choices that align with your well-being. Empowerment is not about perfection; it's about being seen, being heard, and allowing yourself to live authentically. It is about knowing that your past, your pain, and your struggles do not define your worth—they are part of your journey, not the destination.

You are allowed to:

- Take your time to heal. There is no set timeline.

- Feel all your emotions, without judgment. Every feeling is valid.

- Ask for help and accept support. Needing support is strength, not weakness.

- Celebrate small victories, even the ones that feel insignificant. They matter.

- Stand in your truth and live in alignment with your values, identity, and needs.

Remember: your lived experience is not a burden; it is your power. By surviving, seeking help, and learning to care for yourself, you are creating a life that reflects courage, strength, and authenticity. You are more than your struggles—you are a human capable of growth, joy, and connection.

Supporting Someone Experiencing Depression, Anxiety, Self-Harm & Suicidality

Do:

- **Listen without judgment.** Sometimes just being present is the greatest support.

- **Validate their feelings.** Say things like, "I can see this is really hard for you," or "Your feelings make sense."

- **Encourage professional help.** Therapy, counselling, peer support, or medical care can provide essential guidance.

- **Offer practical support.** Help with small tasks, accompany them to appointments, or create a safe space to talk.

- **Check in regularly.** Even a small message or call reminds them they are not alone.

- **Stay calm and steady.** Your presence helps them feel safe when the internal world feels overwhelming.

- **Respect boundaries.** Let them set the pace for talking or acting.

- **Celebrate small wins.** Every step forward, even tiny, is progress worth acknowledging.

- **Learn about mental health.** Understanding their experience shows care and reduces stigma.

- **Create a safety plan if needed.** Know emergency contacts and resources to keep them safe.

✖ Don't:

- **Don't dismiss or minimise.** Avoid phrases like, "Cheer up," "Others have it worse," or "It's all in your head."

- **Don't shame or lecture.** Comments like, "Why would you do that?" or "Stop feeling that way" increase guilt and isolation.

- **Don't force them to talk.** Pressure can make them withdraw further.

- **Don't react with horror or fear.** This can make them feel unsafe to share again.

- **Don't make it about you.** Focus on their experience, not your discomfort.

- **Don't give ultimatums.** Threats rarely help; compassionate guidance does.

- **Don't remove coping mechanisms without support.** Abruptly taking away self-harm tools can increase risk.

- **Don't disappear if they struggle or relapse.** Consistent presence reinforces that they are not alone.

- **Don't assume suicidal thoughts mean they want to die.** Sometimes it's about wanting the pain to stop.

- **Don't compare experiences.** Everyone's mental health journey is unique; comparisons invalidate feelings.

Key Takeaways:

- Presence, empathy, and patience are more powerful than advice or solutions.
- Supporting someone doesn't mean fixing their pain; it means walking beside them in it.
- Healing is possible, even if progress feels slow or uneven.
- Connection, validation, and understanding are lifesaving.

Emergency Resources (Australia):

- **Lifeline:** 13 11 14

- **Beyond Blue:** 1300 22 4636

- **Suicide Call Back Service:** 1300 659 467

- **Kids Helpline (under 25s):** 1800 55 1800

Strategies

The following comprehensive list are from my personal lived experience. Bear in mind what works for one individual isn't necessarily what works for another

I'm a very sensory-oriented person, I find comfort in textures, warmth, and weight. To make things clearer, I've grouped some of my strategies and tools into categories that help me during challenging times. You're welcome to try any that resonate with you, and

I encourage you to also create your own list of what works best for you.

Anxiety	depression	Distraction
Fidgets	Reach out to a trusted person to talk	Listening to music
Rescue remedy	Using distractions	Reading
Using grounding strategies	Have a sleep	Colouring in
Squiddy jacket (weighted hoody with squishes in the cuffs)	Name the feelings and emotions	Beading
Using calming strategies	journalling	Painting
Snug sack (a soft sack to swaddle in)	Using soothing strategies	Watching a movie
Small amounts of caffeine	Swaddle in soft weighted items and cuddle a teddy	Talking to others
Go sit on a swing outside	Burning nice scents/ candles	Cooking/ baking
Do some gardening	Eating chocolate/ something sweet or a warm drink	Puzzle games on my phone

grounding	calming	soothing
Going out for a walk	Meditation	Hugging/ patting the cat

Cold face washer on the back of the neck	Monster energy drinks	Hot long showers
Take off shoes and socks	Deep breaths	Oodies
Connecting with nature	Listen to hypnosis	Soft blankets
Journaling	Having a bath	Weighted blankets
Set small goals	Colouring in	Cuddling and talking to a teddy

Chapter 15: When Survival Turned into Living

Poem: The Shift

I wore my numbness like a shield,

a body locked, a heart concealed.

The world was danger, loud and near,

I learnt to live without a tear.

But cracks appeared, a gentle light,

through therapy's slow, patient fight.

Through loss that freed, through hands that showed,

through peers who carried scars untold.

The numb gave way to floods of feeling,

raw and sharp but slowly healing.

I learnt to breathe, to swim, to stand,

to build my life with my own hand.

The scars remain, but now they show,

the strength it took to rise, to grow.

No longer broken, not defined

by what they stole, but what I find.

Survival once, but now I live,

a self-rebuilt, with more to give.

"I carried the weight of scars I never asked for, yet I found within them a map, one that didn't just show where I had been broken, but where I could begin to rebuild."

For most of my life, I didn't live, I survived. Survival mode isn't life, it's constant vigilance—a body on high alert, a mind scanning endlessly for danger, for betrayal, for harm. Every thought, every movement, every word is filtered through a lens of threat. Emotions are dulled because to feel fully would be unbearable. Joy flattens, grief barely touches, love feels foreign, and laughter seems alien. Numbness and being left with no voice aren't a choice; it's the only way to keep breathing.

Living like this means existing behind glass. You see the world but don't participate; you hear people but don't really listen. You smile, but it's a mask. Even when you're surrounded by people, you are isolated in your own head, watching life rather than being part of it.

Somewhere inside, a spark waits. A small part of me longed to feel differently, to exist differently, to be seen, to be heard, to belong, even when the years of conditioning told me it was impossible.

When Karen left the house, I felt as though the ground had shifted beneath me. Coercive control is a cage you cannot see, a constant erosion of your autonomy and confidence. For years, her voice had been the metronome of my life, dictating my thoughts, my movements, my emotions. Every word she spoke was absorbed and internalized; her criticisms and manipulations became the script I used to measure my worth.

The first night she left, the house was silent. Not the peaceful silence of calm, but the eerie, hollow silence of absence. My body reacted first: stomach twisting, chest tight, hands shaking. I walked from room to room, half expecting her to appear, half expecting punishment. My mind raced through rehearsed excuses I didn't need to make, rehearsed explanations that no one was waiting for.

Coercive control doesn't vanish when the person leaves. It lingers like a shadow that stretches across years of your mind. You question your thoughts: Is this mine or hers? Was that decision really mine, or was it what I had been conditioned to do? For months, I found myself almost calling, almost apologizing, almost shrinking back into the role I had been forced into for so long.

But freedom, once glimpsed, is impossible to ignore. Slowly, I realized I could make decisions without fear. I could go where I wanted, use the phone when I wished, speak when I disagreed. That freedom was terrifying but also exhilarating. For the first time in my life, I could exist independently, untethered from her voice. I could begin to remember my own.

During this fragile time, I met peer workers as part of my care team. These were people who had endured trauma and survived, who had transformed their pain into purpose. They were raw, real, and human—not polished professionals reciting theory, but living proof that survival could be converted into service.

I adored them. I observed their patience, their courage, the way they held space for others without judgment. I was drawn to them like a moth to light. In their presence, I felt seen—truly seen. They understood without explanation; they listened without interruption; they shared their own lived experiences without shame.

I began to understand that the horrible parts of my life—the abuse, the trauma, the shame—did not need to remain hidden or meaningless. They could be transformed into understanding, empathy, and guidance. Watching them advocate, support, and educate others planted a seed inside me. Could I do that too? Could I take my story, all the pieces I thought were broken, and make them matter?

It was this inspiration that led me to TAFE. The spark they ignited made me curious, made me believe that maybe I could turn my experiences into something purposeful. For the first time in my life, I allowed myself to imagine a future where my trauma could be a tool for good.

Walking into the classroom for Certificate IV in Mental Health was like stepping into a new world. Anxiety pulsed under my skin, my hands shook, my fingers fidgeted, and Rescue Remedy sat in my bag—a small talisman against the storm in my chest. Every step toward that door felt monumental.

The first lecture was overwhelming. My mind scanned the room, the other students, the notes, my own bag—anticipating criticism, judgment, mistakes. Then I met the teacher. She was kind, patient, approachable, and unfailingly fair. She didn't see me as fragile or broken; she saw potential. That recognition—someone believing in me before I believed in myself—felt revolutionary.

Week after week, I returned. At first, it was stubbornness alone that dragged me through the door. Soon, it became hunger. I hyper focused on every topic, absorbing trauma theory, mental health frameworks, and recovery models like a sponge. Every lecture held mirrors of my own life—reflections of experiences I had buried or forgotten. I began to name patterns, understand triggers, and see my story in the context of a wider system.

Despite leaving school at Year 10, I excelled in my studies. Each assignment, each test, each practical exercise became a chance to reclaim knowledge I had thought I lost forever. I discovered intellectual capacity I had never allowed myself to trust. I learnt about systems, policies, and approaches to mental health that I could apply not only professionally but personally.

Some units were more difficult than others. The domestic violence section was excruciating. Each case study, each example, hit too close to home. I left the classroom shaking and crying, overwhelmed by memories and emotions. But therapy had given me tools. I didn't run; I didn't hide; I returned. Each trigger became a doorway into self-insight, a lesson in reflection, a chance to understand my own patterns.

TAFE was not just education—it was healing. It was a place where my intellect and my heart converged. Each lecture, each discussion, each reflection was a chance to reclaim pieces of myself that had been dormant for decades. I wasn't just learning about mental health; I was learning about me.

The teacher's consistency was vital. Always available, always fair, always encouraging, she created a safe space that allowed me to grow at my own pace. She challenged me, yes, but she did it with kindness, respect, and belief in my ability to rise. That faith nurtured me in ways I could not yet fully articulate.

Placement was another layer of challenge and growth. I expected empowerment, opportunity, and growth, but instead, I encountered organizational dysfunction, injustice, and outright cruelty toward clients. People already struggling with trauma were treated as though their experiences were their own fault. I watched, powerless at times, rage and grief burning inside me.

I found strength and a voice I once never had. I spoke up about the impact because this passion drove from within. I fought for justice and human rights. I didn't let pride take a sideline; I spoke up to make things right. Because of this, I was given a better placement. Because of this growth and change, I dug deep for strength and stuck at it and stayed.

I had learnt through therapy and TAFE that my voice mattered. That witnessing dysfunction did not mean I had to replicate it. I observed, I reflected, I learnt the type of worker I wanted to become. Placement was fire, and fire forged steel in me. It forced me to confront not only what was wrong in the world but what was right in me.

I came home exhausted each day, physically and emotionally drained. But alongside that exhaustion was clarity. I understood more about empathy, about advocacy, about how to honor a person's story without judgment. I learnt that being broken did not disqualify anyone from helping others; in fact, it could enhance the capacity for understanding.

My final placement reinforced not only that this was the right path for me but also that this was where I was meant to be. It was home—assisting others, advocating, hearing them, validating them, working together to find solutions. I never try to fix; instead, I'm curious and encourage clients to find the answers that live deep inside.

I didn't need to be fake; I just did what I needed the most—I listened deeply, connected, and helped guide them along their paths.

Therapy during this time was the slow undercurrent beneath everything else. My therapist worked in subtle, almost imperceptible ways, planting seeds that could not be uprooted. She offered consistency, safety, and patience, showing me that healing is not explosive—it is incremental.

We worked on triggers, slowly exploring the past in ways that did not overwhelm. Each session built on the last, creating a foundation of trust and self-understanding. Emotional flooding was frequent, intense, and sometimes terrifying. I felt grief like a tidal wave, rage like fire, sadness like a weight pressing on my chest, yet I learnt to sit with it. I learnt that my body, once frozen in survival, could now move, breathe, and feel safely.

She helped me understand the biology of my own brain—how trauma reshapes neural pathways, how survival mode locks the nervous system into freeze, fight, or flight. How, with consistency, safety, and awareness, those pathways can be rewired to allow for living, not just surviving. The learning was both intellectual and visceral. I could feel the changes in my body: tension loosening, heart rate normalizing, breath deepening. I was alive in ways I had never been before.

Survival mode had kept me alive, yes, but living—truly living—was something else entirely. Living meant feeling. Everything returned: joy, grief, fear, love, anger. The sensations were overwhelming at first, like my body had to relearn what it meant to be human. Colors seemed brighter, sounds sharper, laughter piercingly vibrant. Even happiness could feel dangerous because it was unfamiliar.

Setbacks still happened. Dark thoughts lingered, intrusive doubts still whispered, and moments of old trauma tried to reclaim control. But now I had tools, awareness, and perspective. These setbacks were shorter, less consuming, and I met them with self-compassion. I could recognize them as old patterns, not truths.

Parenting changed too. I no longer hovered, no longer wrapped my children in cotton wool. I loved them deeply but allowed them space to make mistakes, to learn, to grow. I no longer blamed myself for every misstep or feared every choice they made. My new internal narrative—one of worth, competence, and love—extended to them. I could parent without fear, without guilt, without shame. No more self-doubt or feeling blame and failure for them when they made their choices (like wonderful teens do) to bend and break rules. I don't scold or yell; I support and guide, let them grow through the mistakes. Home is safe, and I am the safe person—they can always approach me and know I will never judge them.

Looking back, I see the stark contrast between the person I was and who I have become. The child who hid, the adult who survived, the woman who feared her own voice—they are all still there but no longer define me. I am no longer a product of my mother, Karen, or anyone else's narrative. My beliefs are my own, my voice is my own, my life is mine.

Recovery is messy, recovery is slow, recovery is raw—but it is possible. The journey from survival to living, from numbness to feeling, from fear to hope, is tangible, achievable, and profoundly transformative.

I am living, I am worthy, I am enough, and I can continue to grow, to heal, and to thrive.

Chapter 16: The Ones We Think We Know

POEM "The Bed I Never Chose"

I climbed in,

not for love,

not for longing

but for quiet.

For rest.

He whispered comfort

like it was currency,

traded safety

for silence.

I froze.

A child again

in a woman's skin,

trapped between

"don't move"

and "please stop."

He slept,

and I shattered.

On the couch,

I curled my shame,

wrapped it around my daughter

like a blanket.

She came to me unwell

I held her,

but it was me

I was trying to save.

He texted.

As if I'd return.

As if my consent

was still something

he believed he could bend.

I walked away

with tear-streaked glasses

and skin that didn't feel

like mine anymore.

I told the police.

They told me

maybe it was just in my mind.

But my mind

doesn't cry in the shower.

My body

doesn't lie.

I held the truth

like a blade in my throat.

I kept the girls safe

while I bled in silence.

Every school holiday,

I smiled through the wreckage.

Made space for their joy

while mine sat broken

beneath my ribs.

My daughter chose her friend.

I chose her safety.

And I lost more of myself

in the process.

Another rape.

Another scar

stitched into stories

no one wants to hear.

But I am still here.

Not healed.

Not whole.

But holding the line

between love

and survival.

And that,

somehow,

is enough.

"Sometimes the deepest betrayals come from those who held your laughter in their hands."

We met on Tinder—a swipe, a smile, a message—and suddenly I had a secret life. It wasn't scandalous or wild, just mine, quietly, privately mine. Something untouched by judgment or obligation. I didn't want my ex to find out and twist it into something ugly, or for my kids to feel like they had to hide it too. So, I kept it sacred and separate, a pocket of freedom where I could just be… me.

Harry lived over two hours away, which made things feel safer at first, manageable. Every second week, we'd meet somewhere in the middle—a motel, a lake, a walking trail. We both weren't working when we met, so we had time. We used it talking, walking, exploring, laughing like teenagers, dreaming like lovers, healing like two people who thought they'd finally found someone who saw them.

Most nights, we'd fall asleep on the phone. His deep breathing on the line became like a lullaby to me. There was a stillness to those nights, a comfort in the illusion that someone was beside me, hearing my breath, dreaming with me. We shared stories, secrets, scars. He told me about his past, his daughters, the things he wished he'd done differently. I told him about my kids, the chaos of my life, the pieces of me I was trying to glue back together.

We went to Jindara often—it became our spot. We'd meet there for long days that felt like hours. We'd flirt like school kids, daring each other to jump in the cold water, climbing rocks, sharing bad food and better kisses. The sun always seemed to linger longer when I was with him. It felt good, honest, normal. Like maybe I wasn't broken after all. Like maybe I could be loved again, this time gently.

We didn't involve the kids, not really. Until one day, at a local park, we crossed that line. He had two daughters, both a bit older than mine. We agreed to meet "by chance," like strangers. The girls played while we exchanged knowing glances. Our daughters connected quickly, as children often do, unaware of the complicated adult world swirling around them.

That day, something in me softened. I thought maybe, just maybe, this was the start of something real, something safe. But in truth, it was the start of something else entirely. Something I couldn't yet name, something that would later shatter everything I thought I knew about trust, love, and danger.

Because betrayal doesn't always come with a warning. Sometimes it comes wearing a smile and holding your hand at a lake. At first, everything felt mutual, balanced, and equal effort. He had time, I had space, and our lives, though messy, found a rhythm.

But then he got a job. I was happy for him, truly proud even. But his work meant our long, lazy days disappeared. The spontaneous calls became shorter, the sleep phone calls faded. The meetups spaced out, and I began to ache for something that was once easy, once ours. I missed him, or maybe I missed the version of us I had built in my head.

With the distance still there and his availability shrinking, it was me who made the effort. Me who packed the car, rearranged life, and made excuses. I started driving to his place—a choice that became a slow erosion of comfort. He visited me in my area now and then, but I never let him come to my house. I couldn't. Everything still had to be hidden from my ex, from the kids, from the chaos that always seemed to be waiting just around the corner.

When I stayed at his place, I never felt settled. His house was small, neglected—not in a way that made him cruel, just...

careless. The kitchen smelt faintly of rot, the fridge was stained, the bathroom tiles blackened with mould. The first time I stepped into his shower, I left feeling dirtier than when I went in. I'd towel off and try not to gag, then crawl into bed beside him, pretending it didn't matter. Pretending I could keep finding him attractive, even as the cracks began to show.

Our daughters met a few more times. They got on well—easy smiles, Roblox games, and shared secrets. Eventually, they connected on social media, chatting more than we did. For a fleeting moment, that felt hopeful. Like maybe we were merging families, building something.

But then COVID hit, and everything changed. With the lockdowns came restrictions—physical, emotional, relational, and distance. I felt the sting of absence more acutely; he was accepting of it being as it was. The effort, once shared, now lived squarely on my shoulders. It was always me driving, me initiating, me adapting. I began to feel like a ghost haunting his life—a toy, a convenience, a placeholder, a woman filling time between his real priorities.

Almost a year passed like that, a slow unravelling disguised as routine. I stopped feeling excited, stopped laughing as much. I stopped pretending I was okay with doing all the work. I wanted connection, not crumbs. I wanted presence, not obligation. I wanted to be chosen, not just accepted when it suited him.

So, I decided to stop showing up. I didn't make a scene, I didn't beg. I just quietly pulled back—stopped calling, stopped driving, stopped performing. When I told him I was done, that I couldn't carry the weight of both of us anymore, he barely reacted. That hurt more than anything.

Even after I ended the relationship, our daughters stayed in touch. Their bond seemed unshaken, innocent, full of laughter and endless chat threads. Every school holiday, they'd ask for a sleepover, desperate to see each other again, even if the adults behind the scenes were no longer connected.

The first time, I went with Jennifer. I stayed the night but insisted on sleeping on the couch. I didn't want to be close to him. I didn't trust him, not anymore. But I was trying to keep things civil, trying to honour the girls' friendship without putting myself at risk. I stayed in my own space—distant, alert, watching everything and saying little.

The second visit, I met him halfway and let Jennifer go on her own. She was excited, confident, full of trust, and I let myself believe that it was okay. That I didn't need to be there. That he wouldn't cross any lines with the girls, even if we were done.

Then came the third visit—the one I'll never forget, the one that broke everything. I had agreed to take Jennifer again, another sleepover. The girls were giddy, full of plans. I had intended to stay, but on the couch as I had once before. That night, after the kids were tucked into their beds, he looked at me and said quietly, "You'll be more comfortable in my bed."

I said no with my body, but not my voice. I hesitated, unsure, uncomfortable, but he kept at it. "You need a proper night's sleep," he said. "Don't be silly. You'll be better off in the bed than on that hard couch." And I let him convince me.

I didn't know he had a hidden agenda. I wish I had had a gut instinct. Instead, I trusted his words and his intent. I got into his bed, curled as far to the side as I could. I told myself I'd just sleep. That it didn't mean anything. I was safe, and I was still in control. But slowly, steadily, he inched toward me. His hands moved with quiet confidence, not aggression, like he was entitled to me. Like I had no say anymore, and I froze.

Not willing to take part but unable to stop him, my voice locked inside me. My body braced. I didn't respond, I didn't help, I just... endured. He did what he wanted to do and then rolled over and went to sleep. Just like that. No apology, no acknowledgment, no care.

As soon as he began to snore, I slipped out of the bed, heart pounding, skin crawling. I padded back to the couch, feeling used, hollow, and ashamed. I couldn't shake the sensation of him on me, couldn't stop my own thoughts from screaming. I felt filthy inside and out.

Not long after, Jennifer came looking for me. She wasn't feeling well. She curled up into me, pale and drowsy. I took her into the spare bed, wrapped my arms around her, and whispered comfort. But the truth was I was comforting myself too. She didn't know.

She had no idea that just down the hallway, her mother had been violated in silence. That while she giggled and played with her best friend, something was taken from me again—not just my body but my voice.

I lay there with her in the dark, holding her tightly, crying quietly into her hair. I told myself I was strong, that I was protecting her, that I could carry this pain alone. That she didn't need to know.

The next morning, he texted me from his bed: "Come back in here." I stared at the message, my stomach turning. I didn't reply. Instead, I packed our bags in silence—no breakfast, no smiles, no explanations. I left before the sun had fully risen, sunglasses hiding the tears that refused to stop. Jennifer chatted beside me in the car, unaware. I drove, one hand on the wheel, the other clutching my stomach as if I could hold the pieces of myself together.

When I got home, I broke. The shame clung to me like a second skin, but somewhere beneath it, a small, fierce voice told me: This wasn't okay. You didn't deserve that. Say something.

So, I did. I called the police. It took everything I had to pick up the phone. My voice trembled, my hands shook, but I told them. I told them everything—about the bed, about the way he crossed the line, about the way I froze, just like I had all those other times in my life when someone decided my body belonged to them.

They told me to come in and make a formal statement. I jumped in the car and drove before I could change my mind— and did.

I sat there in a room with blank walls and cold chairs and tried to put my trauma into words. Tried to explain what it's like when your voice vanishes, when your body stops responding, when you're awake but unreachable.

I cried, I whispered, I told the truth, and then... they told me maybe it was just in my mind. That maybe I needed mental health support, that what I was describing didn't sound like something they could act on. He wasn't even spoken to. Just like that—dismissed.

I left that station feeling more violated than when I walked in. Another man got away with it. Another person walked free while I carried the weight—and worse, they made me feel like a liar. Like it hadn't happened. Like I was the problem. How do you hold that? How do you breathe through that kind of dismissal, that brutal invalidation, when you've already torn your insides out just to speak?

They gave me a referral to CASA, a sexual assault support service. Another healing journey, they said. Another round of retelling, re-explaining, reopening. But even there… I was too much. Too much pain, too much risk, too unsafe to engage in their therapy. I was shut out, turned away because my trauma was too loud, too complex, too frightening. The message was clear: You're not safe enough to heal here. I wanted to scream—then where the fuck am I supposed to go?

I didn't want to be broken. I didn't want to be the girl with too many scars, too much history, too many ghosts. I just wanted someone to sit with me and say, I believe you, it mattered, you matter. But I didn't get that—not from the police, not from the service—so I carried it on my own again.

I began, slowly, to build something from the ruins—not because I was ready, but because I had no other choice. The hardest part wasn't what he did—it was what I had to do next.

The girls were still talking, still giggling late into the night, still dreaming up the next sleepover. Jennifer had no idea what had happened behind that closed bedroom door. To her, he was still just her friend's dad, the one with the messy house and the loud laugh. The one who made her feel welcome—and I didn't know what to do with that.

How do you protect your child from someone they don't even know they need protecting from? How do you tell your daughter that the man who once smiled at her across the dinner table hurt her mother in a way she can't yet understand? Do you tell her at all?

I brought it to therapy; tears streamed down my face. I couldn't decide. I didn't want to steal her friendship. I didn't want to plant fear. But I also couldn't let her go back there. I couldn't pretend nothing had happened. My therapist listened gently, patiently, and then she offered something I hadn't expected. "I can tell her," she said. "We can do it together. In session."

She had written a scene—careful, age-appropriate, sensitive. She read it to me first, walking me through each line, checking my body language, making sure I was okay. I nodded through sobs, the shame burning hot in my chest, but I agreed—it needed to be done.

In a quiet Zoom therapy session, with soft lighting and steady presence, my daughter heard the truth. Not all the details, not the full weight—but enough. Enough to know that I was hurt, that someone we once knew had done something terrible, and I would need time to heal.

Jennifer was calm, still, brave in a way I hadn't expected. She didn't cry, she didn't ask questions right away—she just took my hand and gave me a hug.

The therapist explained that she could still be friends with her friend, that this didn't have to take everything from her. But she couldn't ever stay at that house again—that boundary was clear. If she ever needed to talk, she could speak to her own counselor in her own time.

She nodded, quietly, thoughtfully, and then she looked at me and said, "I'm sorry he hurt you." I will never forget that moment—that small voice holding more strength than most adults I've known.

She didn't ask me to be okay. She didn't try to fix it. She just saw me. For the first time in weeks, I felt less alone. I tried to keep going, tried to smile, to cook dinner, to answer emails, to fold the washing, to pretend I wasn't crumbling inside. But then I heard my daughter on the phone—she was chatting with his daughter, her best friend, laughing about games and plans and holidays.

When I heard his voice in the background, it hit me like a punch—sudden, raw, paralyzing. That voice. That voice that once whispered fake comfort, then violated me in silence.

I couldn't breathe. My body remembered before my mind could catch up. I wanted to scream, to rip the phone from her hands, and tell her to hang up. But I didn't. I couldn't. Because I knew it wasn't her fault. I didn't want the girls to suffer. I didn't want to punish them for his choices.

Then he had the audacity to contact me and try to speak to me, like nothing had happened.

Like we were still polite acquaintances. Like I was someone he could smile at in passing. I wrote him a message—calm, composed, full of rage:

"You don't get to do what you did and act like it never happened. You don't get to look through me and pretend we're fine. You can't take it back with silence."

I hit send with shaking hands and then I cried. I kept it all to myself—the storm inside me. I didn't tell my ex. I didn't tell my friends. If the police wouldn't believe me, I told myself, why would anyone else?

I didn't want my ex or his daughter back in my home, but I didn't want to break the girls either. So, every school holiday, I agreed. Every time, I hosted her, trying to make it normal for them. The first visit, I ended up in emergency—the thoughts of suicidality were too loud, too sharp, too seductive.

Self-harm, suicidal thoughts—all of it returned like old ghosts, dragging me back into a place I thought I'd finally escaped. But I didn't let anyone see. I wore my mask like armor. I smiled for the girls. I cried into my pillow. Every visit after that, I found ways to survive.

I'd meet his daughter at her mum's house, avoiding him completely. I'd keep busy, keep distracted, keep pretending. I became an expert at staying just functional enough to not fall apart in front of anyone else.

The last holidays broke me in a new way. Jennifer said she wanted to go there—to his house.

She said she didn't care what he'd done to me. That she'd go alone. That he'd never hurt her. That I was overreacting. She couldn't see the danger, couldn't feel what I knew in my bones. I was terrified.

I did the one thing I never wanted to do—I contacted him. Calm, controlled, I told him she was not to come. I told him he was to put a stop to it. He didn't deny it happening. He agreed that she couldn't go to his house—maybe guilt, maybe fear. Thankfully, now I wasn't the villain who stopped her from visiting her friend. The plan changed. His daughter came to stay with us, from her mum's house. Just the girls—no contact with him, no voice, no face, no risk.

I hope it stays that way. I hope the distance keeps growing. I hope the girls drift apart gently, so that no one must bleed to make the break. For now, I carry the weight—quietly, heavily—another rape, another betrayal. Another trauma stitched into the deep scars I already live with—from childhood, from my sister, from Adam, and now from him.

Therapy helps—slowly, painfully. Week after week I show up, even when I don't want to. I've learnt how to survive it, how to live with the wound. But that wound will never close.

I know now: I will never date again. I will never let another man near me.

Love, of any kind, feels dangerous. I can't afford to trust—not anymore. I have taken control where I can. I've kept my daughter safe. I've shielded her from the dark, even when it was swallowing me whole, and maybe… that's the kind of love I can still believe in.

Reflection: - Lived Experience of Adult Sexual Abuse and Assault

Experiencing sexual abuse or assault as an adult can be shocking, disorienting, and painfully retraumatizing. For me, it happened not once, but twice. Each time, it ripped open old, suppressed wounds from my childhood sexual abuse, bringing back memories I had long numbed. The child I had tried to protect and silence suddenly felt present again, and the confusion and pain were magnified.

The disbelief, the fear, and the instinct to freeze were familiar, but this time, I had a choice. I felt a powerful need to speak out and report, to finally release the guilt and shame I had carried for decades from my silence as a child. For years, I had blamed myself for not stopping what happened, for not protecting myself or my sister. As an adult, reporting and seeking justice became a way to reclaim control and reclaim my voice, even though the process was terrifying and often retraumatizing.

Therapy became my lifeline. It gave me a space to face suppressed memories safely, untangle the complex emotions of guilt, anger, and grief, and understand that the abuse was never my fault. It allowed me to see that what I had once numbed—the confusion, shame, and fear—was a survival response, not a failing.

Healing has not meant erasing the past; it has meant reclaiming my body, my voice, and my self-worth. It has meant acknowledging that while the abuse happened to me, it does not define me. I am not broken. I am still here—scarred, yes, but stronger, wiser, and more compassionate toward myself and others.

The silence that once trapped me has become a source of insight and empathy. Where guilt and shame once lived, I now plant understanding, self-respect, and resilience. I have learnt that reporting, seeking support, and speaking my truth are acts of courage, not blame. They are ways to restore the power and control that were stolen.

Hope, and Empowerment for Adult Survivors

Healing from adult sexual abuse does not mean forgetting or erasing the past; it means reclaiming your life on your terms. You can face suppressed truths, unravel the lies you were taught, and rewrite the beliefs that no longer serve you. Therapy, peer support, and safe spaces allow you to:

- **Rebuild trust** in yourself, your body, and in others.

- **Rediscover your self-worth** understanding that what happened to you does not define your value.

- **Allow emotions to return** grief, anger, sadness, and even joy can coexist without shame.

- **Release guilt and blame** these were never yours to carry; they belong to the perpetrator.

- **Learn and grow from pain** your experiences can deepen empathy, resilience, and self-awareness.

- **Reclaim your body and agency** your boundaries, choices, and autonomy can be restored.

Every small step is progress. Speaking your truth, whether privately in therapy or aloud to someone you trust, is a declaration of your power. You may revisit painful memories, feel overwhelmed, or question yourself, but each moment of courage chips away at the power abuse once held over you.

Remember: the child you once were—silenced and terrified—is still within you, but so is the adult who can now witness, protect, and nurture her. You can hold both truths: the reality of what happened and the reality of your resilience. You can say, "This happened to me, but it is not who I am."

Recovery is not about perfection. It is about showing up for yourself each day, claiming your voice, and allowing life, connection, and joy to return. Even after multiple violations, it is possible to rebuild safety, trust, and a life filled with hope. You are not broken; you are alive, you are strong, and you can thrive.

Key Messages for Adult Survivors and Supporters

- **Your silence was survival.** Speaking out now, decades later, does not make you weak, it makes you brave.

- **The abuse was never your fault.** Guilt and shame belong only to the perpetrators.

- **Healing is possible.** Therapy, safe relationships, and reclaiming your voice can restore trust, self-worth, and hope.

- **You are not defined by what happened.** You are defined by your courage, resilience, and the life you choose to build.

- **Support should be survivor-led.** Respect their choices about reporting, therapy, and sharing their story.

- **Reopening old wounds is normal.** Adult abuse can trigger memories from childhood. This is not failure, it is part of processing trauma safely.

Do & Don't List for Responding to Adult Disclosures of Sexual Abuse/Assault

✅ Do:

- **Believe them without question.** Affirm: "I believe you. This was not your fault."

- **Listen with compassion.** Let silence exist; let them guide what they share.

- **Respect autonomy.** Support choices about reporting, therapy, or medical care.

- **Offer practical help.** Ask: "What do you need right now?" instead of assuming.

- **Validate their feelings.** Shock, anger, grief, confusion, or numbness are normal.

- **Maintain confidentiality.** Only share with consent unless legal duty requires otherwise.

- **Encourage professional supports.** Gently suggest therapy, peer support, or advocacy, without pressure.

❌ Don't:

- **Don't question or doubt them.** Avoid "Why didn't you fight back?" or "Why didn't you leave?"

- **Don't pressure them to report.** Reporting must be their choice, in their own time.

- **Don't minimise or dismiss.** Phrases like "At least it's over" or "It could have been worse" are harmful.

- **Don't take over.** Let them make decisions; regaining control is part of healing.

- **Don't gossip or share details.** Their story belongs only to them.

- **Don't assume healing is linear.** Setbacks are normal, patience and presence matter more than solutions.

Key Reminder: Adult survivors often carry the compounded weight of past and recent trauma. By believing, respecting, and supporting them, you help create safety where there was none, and empower them to reclaim voice, control, and hope.

Chapter 17: The Day I Chose Myself

Poem: Choosing Me

I carried wounds no one could see,

A silent ache inside of me.

Tangled roots in broken ground,

A love I lost, but never found.

I bent, I broke, I tried to mend,

A fractured heart with no end.

For years I chased a fleeting ghost,

A mother's love I needed most.

But love that burns with pain and shame

Is not the love that knows my name.

So in the quiet, I found my voice,

And chose myself, my only choice.

The silence came, heavy, cold,

Yet in it, strength began to hold.

I shed the weight, the blame, the lies,

And lifted my own sunrise.

No longer lost in their storm,

I built a place where I am warm.

A home inside, where healing grows

This is the love I now compose.

"Sometimes the bravest thing you can do is choose yourself, even if it means walking away from those who should have loved you unconditionally."

Cutting off my mum wasn't a sudden decision; it was the slow bleeding out of a thousand tiny heartbreaks. A grief not born from loss, but from never having had the thing I so desperately needed in the first place.

She was never a mother to me, not in the way a child deserves. I grew up mothering her: carrying her pain, cleaning up her messes, managing her moods, tiptoeing around her silences, silencing my own voice just to keep peace. I spent my childhood, and most of my adult life, parenting the parent. Always reaching for something I could never grasp: her love, her pride, her protection, but no matter what I did, nothing was ever good enough.

I bent myself into shapes that barely resembled me just to be enough for her. I did everything for her, paid her bills, cleaned up her chaos, defended her, justified her, and kept the family secrets locked tight. I got myself into debt for her, tried to patch over the holes she ripped into everything, and took responsibility for burdens that were never mine to carry. Every time, I was left bruised, emotionally bankrupt, aching, invisible.

There's a certain kind of soul wound that comes from being used by the very person who should have protected you. She didn't just fail me; she trained me to believe her love was conditional. I had to earn it, fight for it, sacrifice for it, but it was never there. Not in any real or safe way. I kept trying anyway because I wanted a mum. I needed a mum. Somehow, no matter how many times she failed me, I hoped she might become one. She didn't, she couldn't, and the longer I stayed, the more damage she caused.

She was toxic; her chaos was a never-ending storm sucking everyone in, spinning truth into lies, turning people against each other, and always emerging as the victim. She weaponized guilt, rewrote history, hurt people, then cried louder than anyone else when they walked away. I was always the one to go back, the one to fix it, to carry the weight so she wouldn't have to, until I couldn't anymore.

There came a moment when I looked at my life, my own children watching me unravel, my body exhausted from holding pain that wasn't mine, my heart heavy with decades of betrayal, and I knew: if I didn't cut the cord now, I was going to bleed out.

So, I stopped answering the phone. I stopped justifying myself. I stopped making excuses for her behaviour. I stopped pretending. I let the silence settle in—heavy, strange, unfamiliar—but it was quieter than the chaos. It was mine, and for the first time, I felt something close to peace.

The breaking point came at Christmas. It had been building all year, but that holiday—always more performance than celebration—broke something inside me. My anxiety was unbearable; I couldn't breathe at the thought of hosting it again, pretending everything was okay, swallowing my truth just to keep the illusion alive.

I did something I'd never done before: I called and cancelled. I said I wasn't doing Christmas; I needed space, peace, a break from the dysfunction. She didn't ask if I was okay.

She didn't offer understanding.

She got angry—not loud-voiced angry, worse—silent, cold, cutting, punishing. While she froze me out, she went straight to my children behind my back, twisting stories and planting seeds. She told them lies, that I didn't care, that I was unstable, that I was cruel. She never even thanked me for the gifts I still sent. That was her pattern: rewrite the narrative, make me the villain, and keep her hands clean. It was textbook manipulation. But it still hurt like hell.

Week after week in therapy, we unpacked her behaviour. My therapist gently labelled it what it was: narcissistic, toxic, emotionally abusive. Words hard to hear, not because they weren't true, but because deep down, I already knew. I just hadn't given myself permission to say it out loud.

"She's not going to change," my therapist said one day. "And no matter what you do, you will never be truly accepted or seen by her." Something inside me cracked hearing that—not because it was cruel, but because it was honest. Sometimes honesty is the kindest thing when you've spent a lifetime wrapped in lies.

I followed her advice. I blocked my mother. I cut off contact. I chose my peace over her power.

Then came the guilt—heavy and unrelenting—like maybe I was the bad one. Like I was ungrateful because she gave birth to me. Because you're supposed to love your mum. Because culture, society, family—they all say cutting off your mother is the ultimate betrayal.

But what do you do when your mother has never loved you? Not in the way love is supposed to feel—safe, warm, unconditional. Her love, if it ever existed, came with conditions, strings, and shame. A trap, a transaction, a performance I was always failing to get right.

And now? Now I feel alone. Now I feel lost. Now I feel confused—like a child abandoned in the middle of a forest, with no way back and no clear path forward. I feel broken in places I didn't know existed. Like somehow this wound is deeper than anything before, because this time, I made the cut. I chose it, and that kind of pain is hard to sit with.

Somewhere, buried beneath the ache, I also feel something else. A quiet kind of strength, fragile, new, still forming. A sense that maybe, just maybe, I am choosing myself for the first time. That protecting my children and myself is the most loving, brave thing I've ever done.

Even when it hurts like hell, I try to move on, try to forget her. Try to convince myself I'm better off, but the truth is it hurts. I miss her—not the woman she was, but the idea of her, the hope of her. The version I created in my mind, the mother I always wished she could be. The one I tried so hard to earn, love into existence, prove myself to—the one who never came.

When Mother's Day rolled around, the guilt took over. I broke the silence. I picked up the phone. I called—not because I wanted to, but because I couldn't bear the shame of not doing it. Because part of me still felt like a bad daughter for protecting myself. Because we're taught to honour our mothers, even when they dishonour us.

But the moment I heard her voice, I knew nothing had changed. She didn't ask how I was. She didn't soften. She didn't acknowledge the distance or the pain between us. Instead, it was the same old demands, the same subtle guilt trips, the same assumption that I was there to serve a purpose—not to be heard, not to be seen, not to connect, but to provide, fix, smooth things over, and give.

I hung up and cried, not because I missed her anymore, but because I finally understood she was never going to be the mother I needed. No matter how many chances I gave her, no matter how much I forgave.

I took the next step. I stopped paying her insurance. I stopped helping her partner—the one she used to replace my father as soon as he passed away. I stopped reaching out. I blocked the numbers. I disconnected every string I'd ever used to try and hold us together.

And still... it hurt! Why did it hurt so much to finally protect myself? Why did I feel like I was the bad one? This was supposed to feel easier, simpler, cleaner.

But the truth? The truth was now I had no biological family left. That sentence alone felt like a punch to the chest—no mum, no dad, no sister, no brother. No one from my bloodline to say, "I see you. I love you. You belong."

I had walked away from all of it, not out of cruelty or anger, but because I had to. To survive. To protect my safety and self-worth. To stop bleeding from wounds that would never heal if I kept letting her reopen them. There's a kind of grief that lives in that choice, not just for the people you left behind, but for the childhood you never had, the family you never got, the love that was never safe or true.

Some days, that grief still finds me—in the quiet, in the holidays, in the empty space where "mum" is supposed to be. My mum showed me, in the end, how little I meant to her. She didn't chase me when I left. She didn't call to ask why. She didn't fight for me.

While I was breaking down, reliving memories, overthinking every word I'd ever said, doubting myself, grieving everything I lost, she just... carried on. Like I was nothing, like I'd never been her daughter, like I never mattered, and maybe that's what hurt most of all.

I couldn't stop thinking about her, wondering if she missed me. If she noticed the silence, if she regretted anything. But deep down, I knew she wasn't thinking of me at all. I wasn't on her mind; I never really had been, not in the way a child should be held in a mother's heart.

Then came the final betrayal, not with screaming or cruelty, but quiet, intentional erasure. The house, the one that was supposed to be mine someday. The one she promised over and over. The place I kept holding in my mind like an anchor, something to one day feel safe in. Gone, taken off the table, without a word, without care. As if it had only ever been a manipulation, a financial investment, a dangling carrot I was never meant to reach.

The life I had planned, the one that helped me justify enduring her chaos, shattered.

There was no reward for loyalty, no comfort at the end of damage. No home, no mother, no belonging. Just silence, just loss, just empty space where something sacred should have been.

And the hardest part? The happiness I thought would come after cutting out toxic people… didn't arrive. No freedom, no relief, no peace—just more isolation, more emptiness, more aching loneliness. I thought removing them would bring clarity, lightness, liberation. But all it did was highlight the absence.

The truth I didn't want to face—even without them, I was still wounded. Still broken, still carrying the scars of everything I'd lived through. I wasn't free. I was alone, and part of me still longed for something that didn't exist—a mother's love, a family's embrace, a future that never had a chance to be real.

Then there was my sister. That loss hit differently, not louder but deeper. More entangled, more confusing. For so long, I carried a quiet guilt that wasn't mine to hold.

She was raped when we were younger, and somehow, I absorbed the shame for her. As if it was my job to carry it, protect her from its weight, to make her life easier in ways I couldn't fix the past. I jumped whenever she needed something: babysitting, favours, money, support. I gave because I believed I owed her—for surviving, for not protecting her, for simply being my sister.

But when it was finally my turn to experience joy, when I became pregnant through IVF after years of longing, pain, and loss, she couldn't be happy for me. She couldn't celebrate with me; she couldn't even pretend. Instead, she said words I'll never forget—sharp, selfish, cutting: "How could I possibly be happy for you when I can't have any more myself?" I stood stunned, breath knocked out of me.

She had eight children, eight, one still a baby in her arms, and here I was, fighting tooth and nail, spending every cent, crying through every hurdle, just to bring one child into the world. One, a child I prayed for, ached for, dreamt of, nd she resented me for it.

She frowned on the way I created my family, mocked it subtly. As if the love I poured into that baby was artificial because it didn't come easy. Because I paid for it. Because I dared want what she already had in abundance.

After that, she began to pull away. Or maybe she had always been pulling, and I was finally strong enough to stop chasing. She cut me out, disappeared, told stories behind my back. She used me as a babysitter when it suited her, then stopped calling when I needed support. She lied to my face, took money without repaying, manipulated every interaction to serve herself.

The truth: she was just like our mum—entitled, a self-declared victim, always the one hurt, wronged, deserving more. Beneath that façade, she was malicious, calculating, cruel in quiet, insidious ways.

She copied everything I did—hobbies, clothes, style, even words, life choices. Not out of admiration but competition, as if my every move was a threat. As if she couldn't stand the idea I might have something she didn't.

Still, I kept trying. I kept hoping she'd change, that we'd heal. That maybe, if we both escaped the damage Mum caused, we'd find each other as sisters—not survivors—but it never happened.

Instead, I lost her too. Suddenly, I was alone. No mother, no sister, no blood ties left that weren't soaked in pain. She disappeared for years—no calls, no texts, no explanation.

Then, out of nowhere, she came back—not with an apology or a changed heart, but needing help. That's how it always went; she only reached out when she wanted something. Always after a few drinks, slurred voicemails, midnight messages. Desperate sobs that felt more performative than real.

Her life had unravelled—her foster kids were removed, her husband moved on without her. She said she was suicidal, that she had nothing left, and of course, I answered. Because that's who I've always been—the one who shows up. The one who tries to fix things, even when the cost is me.

I tried to help. I tried to hold space. I tried to offer a lifeline. But like always, she used me, spat me out when I didn't serve her narrative. Picked me up like an old toy she forgot she had, played with me until bored, then tossed me back into silence. I loved her. I really did. But I hated what she did to me. Hated how her choices scraped across my skin like wounds reopening. How every interaction reminded me that our bond was conditional, performative, manipulative, hollow.

The guilt I carried for years—for not protecting her, for not speaking up about what happened to her—meant nothing to her. She weaponized it when she needed, discarded it when she didn't. She twisted the shame I carried for decades into a tool.

She wanted me to take her children, to step in, fix everything, clean up her mess—but I couldn't. Not this time. I wasn't the one who broke them. It wasn't my job to carry her consequences.

Still, I got involved because I couldn't not care. I helped her kids escape; I supported them through things I had no business being dragged into. Yet somehow, I became the bad guy again. She expected loyalty but refused responsibility. She didn't want to heal; she wanted control. She didn't want to change; she wanted someone to blame.

She kept saying we were the same, but we weren't. We might share blood, trauma, childhood nightmares, but we are not the same. I chose to break the cycle; she chose to become it. I kept wishing for closeness, for a real sister, for connection, for something sacred and safe between us—but it never came.

Just more lies, more manipulation, more empty promises, more pain—and I was tired. I had just begun to accept cutting off my mother—that huge, soul-wrenching decision—and now this? What did it mean that I had to let go of my sister too? What did it mean that the only way to survive was to be completely alone? Why couldn't I just have something simple? Something safe? Why couldn't I be loved without having to suffer first?

The guilt crept in on her birthday. I unblocked her number. I sent a voice message. It didn't come from peace; it came from guilt, longing, that small, hopeful part of me that still wanted a sister.

Even after everything, she still contacts me now and then. Only when she needs something—never to ask how I am, never to show up for me. Always help, always emergencies, always manipulation hidden in fake warmth.

It's a pattern I know too well—the same as Mum. Here I am, alone, no mother, no sister, no blood family left. Just me and the grief of all that was never real. There's a certain kind of grief no one recognizes—the kind reserved for people who are still alive. I grieve my mother, I grieve my sister, not because they're gone, but because they were never truly with me.

It's a strange kind of loss—the mourning of what could have been, what should have been, but never was. I grieve the conversations we'll never have, the apologies that will never come, the closeness I used to ache for but can no longer chase. I grieve the family I was born into, and I honour the truth that biology does not make someone safe or sacred in your life.

Family isn't blood; it's behaviour, its loyalty, it's love that doesn't hurt. Still, I find myself wishing—wishing I had a different life, wishing I had a mum who held me and meant it. A sister who stood beside me, not against me. A family that felt like home, not harm.

I used to think if I just tried harder, loved louder, forgave faster, it would be different. But I've learnt the hardest lesson of all: my mental health cannot survive that kind of pain anymore.

This must be the way it is—not because I stopped loving, but because I started surviving.

Because I chose to stop bleeding for people who never brought bandages. Because I can't keep setting myself on fire just to keep others warm. I still wish people would be proud of me, would see what I've carried, would witness what I've survived. Would stop asking why I don't talk to my family and start asking what they did to me.

Now I am reclaiming something they always stole—the silence. Not the silence of suppression, the silence of peace. I'm letting them go, letting them be. No more chasing, no more fixing. No more rewriting myself to make their stories easier. I'm dumping the blame they put on me. The shame I carried in my body like a birthright—it was never mine to hold.

I am moving forward, not without pain, but with truth. Not with joy, but with clarity. Not because it's easy, but because it's necessary. This is how I survive now—by walking away, even when it hurts. By choosing quiet over chaos, by loving myself enough to say: no more.

Choosing myself wasn't the end of the pain—it was the beginning of healing. It meant learning that love doesn't have to hurt, and family doesn't have to come with strings. It meant stepping into a quiet strength I never knew I had and building a life where I am enough, just as I am. This is my truth, my survival, and my promise to myself: no more bleeding, no more silence, only peace.

Chapter 18: The ADHD Revelation

Poem: "Messy and Magnificent"

I wasn't the loud one,

not the blur in the classroom,

not the runner, the climber,

the chaos in motion.

I was quiet.

Still.

An achiever in silence,

shaking inside

while ticking all the boxes.

I coloured inside the lines

while my mind spilled out

over every edge

unseen, unheard, misunderstood.

They saw the calm

never the storm

beneath my skin.

Perfection is a powerful disguise.

I lost my keys

and forgot the words

but remembered how to smile

when I was crumbling.

I masked like a master.

I earnt praise

while drowning in panic.

I excelled alone

because no one ever taught me

how to ask for help.

Then came the mirrors.

Gentle truths

wrapped in videos and reels.

A therapist planting seeds

in the cracks I'd tried to seal.

Was it ADHD?

Was it trauma?

Or was it both

a tangled thread of

wiring and wounds?

Three days of assessment

and all I got

was retraumatised.

They called it "too complex."

I called it a scream

no one wanted to hear.

Caffeine became my clue.

A drink knocked me out

faster than any sedative.

They said it was placebo.

But I knew.

My body knew.

Still no diagnosis.

Still no help.

Just locked doors

and checklists

I couldn't tick the right way.

I built my own system.

One made of lists

and alarms

and soft forgiveness.

A rebellion in letting myself be late.

A revolution in allowing rest.

I forget things.

I disappear.

I burn out.

I cancel.

I ache to belong

while needing to be alone.

And yet I hold space.

I sense what's not said.

I calm storms that aren't mine

because I know their language

better than anyone.

This isn't failure.

It's a different kind of brilliance.

A jagged, glittering,

non-linear kind of strength.

The world may not understand me.

But I am learning to understand myself.

I am messy.

I am magnificent.

And finally

I believe I am enough.

"I thought I knew what ADHD looked like. Turns out, I was looking in the wrong mirror."

I never thought I had ADHD, not even once. ADHD was for the loud kids, the ones who couldn't sit still, who blurted things out in class, who ran instead of walked, yelled instead of talked. ADHD was wild, chaotic energy, not someone like me.

I was the quiet achiever, the one who sat still, didn't speak unless spoken to, tried too hard to be invisible. I was anxious, driven, always trying to get things done, but only after I'd already cried about it, panicked, and avoided it for a week.

Looking back, the signs were always there. In kindergarten, I barely spoke. I watched the other kids play but didn't know how to join in. No one noticed, no one asked why I kept to myself. I wasn't disruptive, so I wasn't a problem. In primary school, I never put my hand up, I never asked questions, I stayed quiet, hoping no one would call on me. I wasn't lazy or disinterested; I was terrified of being wrong, terrified of being seen.

By secondary school, I taught myself how to survive by overachieving. I threw myself into projects with hyperfocus, often producing A-grade work that stunned my teachers, but it was always done alone. I didn't work in groups, didn't ask for help, didn't collaborate—I just worked harder. The pressure to be perfect consumed me. I excelled at everything except P.E., and even then, I still pushed myself to participate, even though I hated it.

Every job I ever had, I taught myself. I watched, I mimicked, I trialed and errored my way through until I could do it faster and better than anyone else. No formal training, no asking for guidance, just perfectionism and pressure.

On the outside, I looked successful, capable, focused, but inside, I never felt smart. I didn't trust my abilities; every achievement was met with self-doubt. I could never rest in it, never feel proud; the bar was always higher.

Masking became second nature. OCD patterns crept in—aim high, do more, don't let anyone see you fall apart. I exhausted myself trying to be everything to everyone while silently doubting if I was anything at all.

Then came therapy, and with it, the quiet suggestion from my therapist: "This reel reminded me of you." "I wonder if this feels familiar?" No pressure, no judgment, just small seeds gently planted. At first, I brushed it off—ADHD wasn't me. I wasn't hyper, I wasn't loud. But the videos were hauntingly familiar. Women talking about losing their keys ten times a day, putting things in the freezer that didn't belong there. People losing track of time, forgetting appointments they were excited for.

People striving for perfectionism and then collapsing at home after masking all day.

There was one that hit me in the chest: "I don't have a lack of motivation. I have too many tabs open and they're all freezing." That was it. That was me.

Suddenly, my life made sense—the hyperfocus, the shutdowns. The chaos and the clarity, the procrastination, getting things done too early out of fear I'd forget. The overwhelm when plans changed, the shame when I forgot the simplest tasks. Underneath it all was the desperate need to fit in, to keep up, to hold it together.

Maybe I hadn't considered or seen ADHD because I'd been too busy surviving. Maybe I was too good at masking. The more I researched, the more I grieved—for the little girl who thought she was stupid, for the teen who thought her worth depended on output, for the adult who still believed she wasn't enough, confused and uncertain.

This wasn't about a label; it was about finally having language and understanding who I really was—about seeing myself with compassion instead of criticism and understanding how my brain really worked.

My therapist encouraged me to take it further, to see a psychiatrist who worked with adults. Maybe they could confirm it, medicate it, and validate what I was beginning to see. But the psychiatrist barely listened. She skimmed the surface and offered a script I'd heard before: "Let's treat the depression and anxiety first. Deal with the trauma, then maybe, if symptoms persist, we'll look at ADHD."

It felt like another dismissal, another way of saying: "Cope better, mask harder, come back when you're more broken." I left that appointment feeling small, unheard, blocked. I was ashamed for asking, ashamed for hoping. Was I imagining it? Was it all just trauma?

My therapist then suggested a private assessment, so I paid thousands of dollars, hoping this time would be different and I would be heard and seen. Three full days of clinical questioning, tick boxes, judgments, her perceptions, paperwork, interviews, and tests.

I was retraumatized. Flashbacks hit me hard. Questions pulled memories from places I'd sealed shut. I was exhausted, shaken, and completely overwhelmed. I was trying to make sense of what belonged to trauma and what belonged to ADHD.

I was tortured day and night, my mind spinning as I tried to tease apart the strands. Was my forgetfulness ADHD or trauma? My need to mask, to fix, to fawn—what part of me did that belong to? I didn't know anymore, and no one seemed to want to help me find out.

The result? "Too complex to diagnose." "Work on trauma and revisit." Again, no diagnosis, no help, no answers. Just further confusion, abandonment, pointing out that I was too difficult and unable to assist any further. This was meant to give clear answers, to help me find my true identity; instead, it added another layer of trauma and a gap where I wasn't able to be filled or seen.

Then something strange happened—I had an energy drink one afternoon. Expecting a buzz, instead, I passed out. It calmed me, silenced the noise, and helped me to function rationally. The next day, coffee did the same—it made me sleep. One shot, and within 20 minutes, I was slouched over, struggling not to go to sleep.

I started experimenting. Each time, caffeine brought calm, clarity. Sometimes it knocked me out; sometimes it gave me just enough to function. I tried to tell myself it was placebo, but I knew. I'd read about paradoxical reactions in ADHD brains, and it fit perfectly.

Still, no one would listen—too much trauma, not enough certainty. No ADHD diagnosis, no access to medication. No NDIS support, not enough boxes ticked. The system was broken, and I was trapped inside it. Frustrating and heartbreaking all at once, as I struggled to improve my mental health. I was alone, unheard, unseen, and no one was willing to help or support me.

Once, in survival mode, I could do everything. Now, just living day to day, I struggle. I forget the washing, lose my phone, misplace my keys. I'm always late and struggling to function. I people-please until I disappear. I crave connection but cancel plans. I want to be seen but am terrified of being known.

Procrastination cripples me, then I hyperfocus until I burn out. Socializing drains me; loneliness eats me. I want to be alone and yet desperately want to belong. I forget what I'm doing while I'm doing it. I walk into rooms and stand there blank, wondering why I came in. I rehearse conversations in my head but forget my words when they matter. I lose track of time; I lose track of myself.

Every day is a balancing act I never trained for, and through it all, I keep adapting. I build workarounds that make sense only to me—color-coded calendars, endless to-do lists, alarms that I snooze but still set anyway. I give myself permission to be messy, to forget, to feel.

I've stopped apologizing for being late and started thanking the people who wait. I've started asking for accommodations instead of punishing myself for needing them. I've started unlearning the shame that was never mine to carry. I've started giving myself credit for trying, for showing up, for staying alive.

It's confusing, this messy, tangled mix of trauma and ADHD, of strengths and struggles that don't fit neatly into any box. I'm learning to accept what I can't control and to do what works for me, not what others tell me I should do. Writing lists helps me hold my scattered thoughts; allowing myself to be late is a quiet rebellion against impossible expectations. I'm starting to see the superpower in this wiring—a deep empathy, a calm in crisis, an ability to hold space for others even when I'm falling apart inside.

I know what it's like to unravel quietly, to feel invisible in a loud world. But I also know what it's like to hold someone else's pain with steady hands—to sense what's not being said, to love deeply and fiercely because I know what it feels like to be misunderstood.

I'm frustrated by the barriers in the system and the lack of medication to help me find balance, but I'm working with the gifts I have, doing the best I can. Some nights that means drinking dirty chai to finally fall asleep, embracing whatever small comfort I can find. This is my path—imperfect, complicated, but uniquely mine.

While the system may have failed me, I'm learning that I don't have to keep failing myself.

I am allowed to honour the way my brain works. I am allowed to take up space in a world that told me to shrink. I am allowed to be both messy and magnificent, and I'm finally learning to believe it.

Reflection: - lived experience, Living with ADHD

For years, I thought I was lazy, stupid, forgetful, or broken. I carried frustration, shame, and blame, isolating myself from others and believing I was simply failing at life.

I masked endlessly to fit in, mimicking behaviours I thought were "normal," hiding my struggles so that no one would see the chaos and overwhelm inside me. I thought I had to pretend to be someone I wasn't just to be accepted.

When ADHD was finally presented to me, it opened my eyes. Suddenly, the pieces made sense—the constant restlessness, the racing thoughts, the impulsivity, the hyperfocus, the forgetfulness. It wasn't that I was broken; it was just the way my brain worked.

I realized I am neurodivergent, and that is perfect as I am.

Caffeine, therapy, and self-understanding helped me manage challenges, but more importantly, I began to recognize the strengths ADHD brings—creativity, quick thinking, problem-solving, adaptability, and a perspective that sees solutions others might miss.

My brain is not a disadvantage; it's a superpower, and I am normal just as I am.

Masking had been exhausting. It took energy to hide who I truly was, to fit into a world designed for neurotypical brains. Now, I allow myself to step back from pretending and embrace my authentic self. I no longer see my differences as flaws but as part of my brilliance. I am learning self-compassion, self-acceptance, and the joy of being able to simply be me.

Hope, Resilience, and Empowerment

Living with ADHD is not about perfection—it's about understanding yourself and embracing your unique strengths.

Your neurodivergence does not make you less; it makes you different, creative, and capable in ways the world often overlooks.

Challenges exist, yes, but they are not a reflection of failure—they are opportunities to find new strategies, build resilience, and learn more about yourself.

Every step forward, no matter how small, is a victory.

Allow yourself to take breaks, celebrate achievements, and lean on support when needed. The world may not always understand, but self-knowledge and self-acceptance are your greatest tools.

You are enough, exactly as you are.

Supporting Someone with ADHD – Do's & Don'ts

 **DO:**

- Listen and observe without judgment. Understand that distractibility, impulsivity, or hyperfocus are part of how they experience the world.

- Validate their experiences: "I see how hard this is for you," or "I understand why that feels overwhelming."

- Encourage self-advocacy for accommodations at work, school, or in daily life.

- Offer practical support, organisation tips, reminders, or breaking tasks into smaller steps, but only if welcome.

- Celebrate strengths like creativity, quick thinking, problem-solving, and innovation.

- Be patient; ADHD can make time management and follow-through challenging.

- Encourage safe coping strategies like exercise, mindfulness, planning tools, or therapy.

- Respect masking boundaries, let them disclose and engage on their own terms.

- Learn about ADHD to understand behaviours without judgment.

✖ DON'T:

- Don't assume laziness, stupidity, or carelessness, ADHD behaviours are not intentional misbehaviour.

- Don't pressure them to "just focus" or "try harder", these statements increase shame.

- Don't criticize or ridicule; negative feedback reinforces masking and isolation.

- Don't compare them to neurotypical standards, everyone's brain works differently.

- Don't take distractions or impulsivity personally; they are part of the condition.

- Don't force masking to stop; allow them to reveal their neurodivergence safely.

- Don't ignore their coping strategies; even unconventional methods may be crucial.

- Don't minimize struggles; ADHD can be exhausting and overwhelming.

Key Message:

Supporting someone with ADHD is about **patience, validation, and celebrating differences**. Their brain may work differently, but it brings **strengths, creativity, and unique brilliance** that deserve recognition, understanding, and respect.

Chapter 19: The Safe Place That Disappeared

Poem: I Entered, I Gave, I Let Go

I stood at the door with trembling hands,

A storm in my stomach, too loud to stand.

My voice rehearsed a dozen ways to hide,

But fear walked me in, though part of me died.

A gentle face, a warming cup,

A quiet space where time slowed up.

I sat in silence, colouring pain,

Found myself breathing, feeling again.

They welcomed my stillness, accepted my tears,

Built me a place that softened the years.

With each craft shared, with each thread spun,

A new kind of safety had quietly begun.

I taught, I gave, I helped others create,

Wove joy from trauma, reshaped fate.

From diamond dots to lanyard strings,

I built a home from broken things.

We hid tiny ducks, we laughed through the grey,

We found meaning on Orphans' Christmas Day.

Bill's stories, Bianca's care

We built something real, something rare.

But the winds shifted, cold and fast,

And the warmth we'd nurtured didn't last.
Rules replaced kindness, clipboards took hold,
And hearts once open turned distant, cold.
I was labelled, blamed, misunderstood,
For accepting the care they once said I should.
The gift of support turned into a weapon,
And all I had offered was suddenly questioned.
Two against one in a sensory room,
No space for my voice, just quiet doom.
Branded unstable, too much, too wrong,
They forgot how I'd held them all along.
I left with my truth, my back to the door,
Grieving the place that wasn't mine anymore.
But I walk with my values, not shame or despair,
Knowing my soul still lingers there.
Because I entered scared, and I gave my heart,
I built connection, I played my part.
And though they turned cold and shut me out,
I walk away stronger, without a doubt.
With head held high and spirit intact,
I know my worth and I won't go back.
Somewhere out there, there's space for me still,
A place that aligns with my voice and will.

"Some spaces save us not with treatment, but with tenderness. And when they go, they leave a silence louder than pain."

It began with a pamphlet. A folded, creased flyer passed to me by Harper during a session. "You might like this place," she said, her voice soft with suggestion, not pressure. I remember running my fingers over the paper, unsure what I was looking at. It was simple, just words and a logo. But what it offered was something I hadn't dared hope for: a safe space. A place I could just be.

CONNECTED STEPS HUB was a quiet, peer-run wellness hub, no wrong door. No need for an appointment, no shame for how you showed up. I didn't need to be fixed, I just needed to exist without fear, and for a while, that's exactly what CONNECTED STEPS HUB gave me.

The drive there on my first day was hell. My stomach churned, and my heart pounded against my ribs. I was rehearsing in my head what I could reveal, what I should say. I was terrified of saying too much or not enough, of crying uncontrollably or being ignored. Even as the automatic doors opened, I wanted to turn and run.

My feet felt glued to the floor, my head was loud, so loud I could barely hear anything else. I felt nauseated, like I might throw up. I was panicking about losing control or saying the wrong thing.

Isla, a peer support worker, greeted me with calm eyes and a gentle energy. She offered me a warm drink and walked me around, but it was like I had my head underwater. Her words sounded muffled, and nothing sank in.

It wasn't until I sat with her one-on-one in a quiet corner that her voice started to reach me. Her bubbly nature slowly chipped away at my panic. I colored in for a distraction as I spoke. This helped me to avoid eye contact or overthink the words I wanted to say. By the time I stood to leave, I felt lighter. I felt reassured and planned my schedule to visit more regularly. The shift while at the visit that day made me feel safe enough to plan my return home now, with less heavy dark thoughts; instead, they were replaced with light and hope.

In those early visits, it felt like stepping into a warm hug. The kind of place where the very air wrapped around you like a blanket. As you left, you could almost see a rainbow arcing above the door. Not literally, but in spirit, hope lingered in the walls. The moment you crossed the threshold, it was like your burdens weighed a little less. Moments of joy and laughter would creep in, a smile even come across my face.

Over the weeks that turned into months, CONNECTED STEPS HUB became more than a drop-in center. It became a sanctuary, a place that remembered my name. The staff saw the exhaustion behind my eyes and made space for it. Some days I joined in activities; other days I just sat in silence with a hot drink and tried to steady my breath. There was no pressure to talk, no shame in needing quiet.

Craft sessions became the heartbeat of many of my visits. There was always something to do with your hands, something that distracted the noise in your mind. Diamond art, paint by numbers, jewelry making, card making. I donated a wide range of supplies and watched them bring joy and focus to the space. I wasn't just a participant; I was a contributor. I taught others how to thread, knot, and craft with care. I introduced vision boards, created collages, and painted little pots with fake plants inside. We made coasters as a community project with smiley faces that became part of the décor. I brought in fidgets, magnets, handmade lanyards—all colorful and soft, each one designed with intention. Staff and guests started wearing them proudly. They were more than accessories; they were symbols of identity and belonging.

Craft was connection. It gave us space to speak truth without filters because our hands were busy and our guards were down. Around those tables, people came alive, voices soft spoken, stories told. I often planned and facilitated these sessions silently in the background, allowing others to take the lead, but I was always present. My energy was there in every brushstroke, every bead, every idea born from a need to make this place feel like home.

The CONNECTED STEPS HUB was a place of fun and laughter. You could walk in feeling depressed, and by the time you left, you had connected, engaged, and for a moment, forgotten the heaviness. We even had hidden treasures—tiny silicone ducks smuggled in and hidden throughout the space. Finding one sparked joy and mystery. "Where are they coming from?" became the inside joke. Laughter echoed around the room, smiles on faces that once displayed doom and gloom.

Then came the friendships. Hazel was one of the first. She was a trans woman who just got me—sharp-witted, compassionate, someone I clicked with instantly. We started catching up outside of CONNECTED STEPS HUB—coffee, long chats, checking in. She became a best friend. Matilda was another, a widow carrying deep grief. On her husband's anniversaries, I'd spend the day with her so she wasn't alone. We shared stories, soup, and the weight of memory. Bree was neurodiverse, with a vibrant, tender spirit. I could see her meltdowns coming before they hit. I sat with her through the waves, helped her breathe through them. I felt her. She felt me.

When Christmas came and CONNECTED STEPS HUB closed, we didn't want to be alone. So, we created our own gathering—an Orphan's Christmas in the park. Everyone brought a plate. I made deconstructed trifle, mini muffins, jelly cups, fruit, spray cream, UHT custard. It was a hit. We laughed, swapped stories, shared tears, and bonded more deeply. That day changed things. It was raw, real connection—a patchwork family created through shared pain and mutual understanding. That day was about presence, not celebration, and it gave me the deepest sense of belonging. The first Christmas that was bearable, not lonely, and I know the others felt the same way too.

Bill was the heart of CONNECTED STEPS HUB in those early days. He wasn't just a coordinator; he was a lighthouse. When he saw how far I traveled to attend, he offered to support me over the phone. He gave me his email for when the center was closed. He told me to bring my child if that made it easier. He even offered to walk beside me into services I was too scared to face alone. He shared his own story—childhood trauma, DV—and I saw myself in his words. He made me feel seen. He didn't just hear what I said; he understood the things I couldn't find the words for. He validated my experience and helped me build safety plans, offered resources, and reminded me that I wasn't alone. He made me feel worthy of healing.

Then it changed. Hopeville pulled out from funding, and Fast-forward stepped in. Bill oversaw the transition and then he left. Bill was the heart of the CONNECTED STEPS HUB; his departure saw the once safe space slowly fall into a place of mismanagement and dysfunction.

Isla moved from peer support to manager. Her skills in peer support were amazing, but as a manager, power went to her head. Isla, once kind, caring, and compassionate, moved to this cold, stern, emotionless monster. She used ChatGPT for how to manage situations because she had no clue how to negotiate or de-escalate situations, and everything shifted. The air thickened with policies, from non-clinical to clinical; guests lost their name and became data and statistics. Smiles were replaced with clipboards, tick sheets, and rigid boxes to fit into.

What once felt like family now felt like performance. One day someone said, "This place is like a speed-dating pick-up spot now. People are sleazy and say they're going to work the room." I laughed, but inside I ached because that's not what it was meant to be.

I was invited onto the LEAG board. I was proud; I believed in it. I fought to protect what we had—for the changes to stop, for the guests to have a voice in the space we used, to be able to feel included and safe on all levels. But one by one, the soul of the place was stripped away. New guests became loud and dominant; the old guests absorbed into the walls. Peer support workers became professionals, and fewer connections were being formed.

I had stepped away for a while, grieving the loss of Harper. Her sudden silence—the rupture of our therapeutic bond—left me reeling. I didn't hate her, but I was confused, heartbroken, and longing for answers.

Returning to CONNECTED STEPS HUB felt like the only place I had left to ground myself. But it seemed that grief was now weaponized. Isla and Bianca had worked with her; I couldn't shake the feeling that maybe they talked behind my back. That maybe my pain was seen as instability.

I was told I was breaching boundaries, that I expected special treatment. That I wanted more than what others got, but I never asked. It was always offered—the emails, the phone support.

That wasn't me demanding; it was them extending care. I was always checking: "Am I too much?" "Is this okay?" And I was always told, "You're fine." But that reassurance turned to accusation; the very things they once praised were now used against me.

Then came the final visit. My social anxiety was unbearable, but I forced myself to show up. I sat in the corner, doing diamond art with trembling hands—just trying to be there, trying to show myself I could regulate, participate, connect.

Isla approached. "I need to speak to you in the sensory room," she said. I said no. Quietly, for once, I used my voice.

But she insisted. Inside the sensory room, Bianca was already waiting. Two staff, one of me. I felt trapped and overpowered by dynamics.

I dissociated, staring at the door wanting out, unable to hear any of their words. They accused me of being inappropriate because of a gift Hazel had given Bianca: a bear and bracelet. Gifts I had asked her to get were meant to be funny and humorous. A gesture of thanks and feedback for a good job quickly turned sour and thrown in my face. The gifts chosen were personal, and that wasn't my choice. The gifts were then seen as invasion and not a joke between us.

A small, sweet moment turned into something ugly. No one asked my side, nor did they reveal what the gifts were. Instead, they handed back a bag and said, "I can't accept them." That was the first I had seen of them; they weren't what I asked Hazel to get, and they weren't what I would have purchased. My idea was humor—flying ducks and fidgets. These clearly didn't have my name on them, yet they were now attacking me.

They just told me how wrong I was. I couldn't speak; my voice was gone. "Can I go now, please?" I asked, barely audible. I walked out in tears. I got in my car, blasted music to drown my pain, and cried all the way home. I called Hazel and told her what happened. She said she wouldn't go back either.

I sent a final message to explain—to use the voice I had lost under threat in that room—to clarify the misunderstanding and what was meant to have been purchased. It didn't matter. I was already branded: unstable, inappropriate, too much.

CONNECTED STEPS HUB was gone—everything I helped build, everything I gave—erased. The "no wrong door" promise was a lie. Trauma-informed care became nothing more than a slogan. The real trauma came from being silenced, called problematic, and not supported.

The board became more about being told of change and outcomes instead of being asked opinions and given options to speak. Budgets were being blown out, spent on plants, paint, rebranding. Guests became data points and statistics, guinea pigs watched instead of supported. It wasn't a community anymore; it was just toxic.

I was left spiraling, alone, suicidal, grieving the loss of a space that had once helped me find myself. I hated being labeled. I hated feeling like a problem. I hated that every safe space seemed to end in the same kind of betrayal.

But this time something is different—I see it clearly now. I did nothing wrong. I gave, I tried. I stayed true to my values; I carried integrity even when no one else did. I protected people, created beauty, brought light into that space.

When they stopped seeing me, I didn't stop seeing them. No, I won't go back—not because I'm bitter, but because I know I deserve better.

This loss was their failure, not mine. I still grieve, I still ache. But I walk with truth now and with the knowledge that the person I am—the person who brought color, care, and community to CONNECTED STEPS HUB—is someone worth protecting.

Chapter 20: When He Came Home a Man

Poem: Roots and Wings

I held you close before you knew

the world could break a soul in two.

I vowed to be the love you'd need,

a shelter strong, a steady creed.

I gave you roots to ground your feet,

and wings to chase your dreams, complete.

But flying storms and reckless skies

came with fire in your young eyes.

You changed from boy to stranger fast,

a shadow of the past I grasped.

Selfish, wild, with roads unowned,

and risks you took… all alone.

You lead the lost, you chase the night,

forgetting home, forgetting right.

Your freedom's edge is sharp and thin,

a battle lost I cannot win.

Yet still my heart will not let go,

though pain and fear have learnt to grow.

I love you fierce, but hold my ground,

in silence deep, in whispered sound.

You are not me, your path your own,

your heart a place I've never known.

But I am here, unbroken, strong

a voice to guide you through the storm.

Roots and wings, love and loss,

the cost of care, the lines we cross.

And if you fall, or fly too far,

I'll still be here, your northern star.

"I gave him roots. I gave him wings. I just never knew how much it would hurt to watch him fly into a storm."

I raised him from six months old, not as a temporary carer, not as a foster placement, but as my son. From the moment I held him in my arms, I made a silent promise that he would never feel the things I had felt. He would never go without, never feel unloved, unwanted, or unsafe. I wanted to give him the kind of childhood I had only ever dreamt of—soft, warm, and certain. A home where he could grow and become whoever he was meant to be.

And for years, I did. Through scraped knees and bedtime stories, school lunches and hard conversations, I showed up. I protected him from the DV of his biological brother. Despite all the hurt from him, he continued to idolize him. He had a stronger, safer bond with his little sister, always helpful and playing fun games with her. My heart melted when I saw the compassion he would bring, and his little imagination with Santa and the tooth fairy.

I wrapped him in all the love I never had. I protected him like my life depended on it, because in many ways, it did. He was mine in every way that mattered—not by biology, but through every midnight feed, every parent-teacher meeting, every time I stood between him and the world. I gave him all of me, the healed parts and the broken ones, and raised him as if he had come from my own womb.

But foster care doesn't always honor that. The system is colder than the love that raised him. To them, I was just a career, a step in his path, a babysitter, paperwork, a placement, a file, and a number. But to me, to us, we were a family chosen by love, not forced by blood.

Then he turned eighteen, and when he came home, he didn't return as the boy I once carried. He walked through the door taller, older, layered with a life I hadn't been there to witness. His voice was deeper, his eyes held stories I hadn't heard. He came back not as my child but as a man, off the rails, with adult demands and a fractured history still stitching itself together.

I wanted to hold him, but I didn't know how anymore. The space between us had grown, filled with unspoken hurts, years of restrictions that limited my parenting, and systems that stepped between love and legality. Still, I tried. I kept showing up, just like I always had. Because no matter how old he gets, no matter how far he roams, I will always be the one who raised him with the kind of love I never received—even if he never fully understands what that cost me.

I tried so hard to be the opposite of the parents who raised me. I was present, attentive. I made sure he had rules and structure, not as punishment but as a framework for safety. I allowed him to make mistakes and learn from them, knowing the world outside wouldn't be as forgiving. I didn't hover, but I never disappeared. I wanted him to feel safe in the way I never did.

When he told me he wanted to leave school, I didn't fight him. He had a full-time job lined up on a farm he adored, surrounded by cows, dogs, and early sunrises—a rhythm that seemed to settle something restless in him. He was thriving out there, or so I thought, so I agreed. I supported his decision because that's what you do when you're raising a man—you let him find his footing, even when your heart braces for the fall.

At seventeen and a half, he moved out, and just like that, the house changed. Quieter, emptier—not in a peaceful way, but in a way that echoed. It was too soon for goodbye, but it felt like the beginning of one.

His eighteenth birthday was approaching, a milestone I had carried in my heart for years. I wanted to give him something unforgettable—a memory, an experience to mark his passage into adulthood, a celebration of how far he'd come, and of all the parts of him I'd fought to protect. I wanted to give him what I never had, and what I never got to experience with his brother—but he refused.

No party, no gathering, no fuss. He said it didn't matter to him. I tried to respect that, even though it broke my heart. I tried not to take it personally, even though everything in me wanted to say, don't you see how much this means to me?

Then, while I was away for the weekend, eight hours away, he threw the party anyway. He waited until I was gone, invited everyone. He called me that night, drunk, slurring, vomit on his shirt—a mess before the sun had even set. I was eight hours away, helpless, staying on the phone with him as my heart quietly broke all over again.

All I wanted was to celebrate him. All I wanted was to be there. But he didn't want me there, and that really hurt. It felt like rejection, abandonment—the kind I experienced as a child, only this time I was an adult and it was from my child.

A few weeks later, he told me he was done with the farm. The early mornings, the long hours—it wasn't for him anymore. Just like that, he wanted to come home, and of course, I said yes.

Because love doesn't keep score, even when it hurts. I was the mum who would always be there, support and never judge. I wanted him to know he could come to me for safety, no matter what was going on.

But something had shifted. This return wasn't like a child limping home with a scraped knee. This was a young man who'd tasted independence and now returned half-grown, half-lost, full of pride and confusion. I, as always, was still his landing place, someone who loved unconditionally and provided a safe space.

Even when he pushed me away, even when it stung— because real love stays, even when the door keeps swinging both ways. The choices he was making weren't great ones, but I wasn't there to tell him that, as it's his journey to ride out.

I poured myself into preparing his return—it was the only thing I could control. I gave up my craft room, my sacred space, the place where I stitched myself back together. I packed it all into boxes and moved it into the shed, sacrificing what fed my well-being so he could have what he wanted.

I spent thousands on the furniture he chose—the bed, the TV, the sleek black décor, masculine, minimalist, grown-up. I created the room he said he wanted—not just a bedroom, but a whole new beginning.

I poured my heart into it, but the man who came home was no longer the boy I raised, and if I'm honest, I no longer knew him. He was broader now, his voice deeper, his eyes had changed. There was a hardness I couldn't reach—a lost soul, thrill-seeking behaviors, not sleeping, always out heading for trouble. He was polite enough, said thank you, but the warmth, the connection, the soft thread of love that had always tied us together... it felt frayed, almost gone.

I stood in the doorway as he dropped his bag with barely a glance at all I'd done. No smile, no comment, just a nod, like it was expected and he was just entitled. That's when I realized:

I had built a room for a son I no longer recognized. The boy I once knew—reasonable, reliable, someone I trusted—had shifted. He became selfish, entitled, and all about himself.

He showed no respect for people or the law; he took endless risks on our roads with bikes and cars. He wasn't here at home with me or his sister. Instead, always out with his mates, so much younger than him, meant everything to him, and he was leading them astray. He didn't care about the consequences; he didn't care about me.

He was spiraling, and I was trying—trying to help, to guide, to hold on. But it felt like speaking through glass; every word I spoke was ignored or blocked out. He came home, but not to stay—not really. He rarely slept here. He would come, shower here, eat here, but his life happened somewhere else.

Gone most nights till 3 a.m., out with teens I didn't know. Riding motorbikes, running from police, no helmet, no license. No fear of risk or consequence—it was chaos masked as freedom. He did as he pleased—no rules, no regard, no accountability.

He treated me like I didn't matter, like I was just someone to take from. He came in, showered, blasted music, ate whatever he wanted, dumped his dirty laundry, and disappeared again. The bills piled up—electricity, food, heating—but he contributed nothing. Not a dollar, not a gesture, yet he asked for money, for cigarettes, to be picked up or dropped off at the last minute.

Still, I loved him. Still, I worried because the boy I had raised with such fierce care had become someone I didn't know how to reach. He bought a car—no license, no registration, no insurance—another risk layered onto a life already spiralling.

I could see the headlines before they were written; my stomach churned; my heart wouldn't rest. He thought he was invincible, above the law, smarter than the rest. But I knew how these stories end, and I refused to sit back and watch.

I used my voice, the one I fought so damn hard to find. I stopped walking on eggshells. I stood in the truth, no matter how much it hurt, and I went to the police. Not to punish him, not to shame him, but to try one last time to save him. The guilt clawed at me, the ache of betrayal, but the fear of losing him… that was louder.

Maybe being caught would be his wake-up call. Maybe it would break the illusion of invincibility. Maybe, just maybe, he'd see that I wasn't doing this to him; I was doing it for him, because I still believed in who he could be.

He isn't me; he didn't start life broken like I did. He had love, safety, security—and maybe that's why it's so hard to watch him throw it all away. I envy the chances he has, the chances I never did. I wish I could shake the truth into him: "Don't ruin this, don't ruin yourself, don't make me bury my son."

But I can't force insight. All I can do is love him—not blindly, not at the cost of myself—but with boundaries, with honesty, with open hands and a strong spine. Because he may be an adult, but he's still acting like a child—reckless, unsafe, untouchable.

I'm still a mother—broken-hearted, brave, and holding the shattered pieces of the boy I once knew. I let him be him, and I let me be me. I won't silence myself for his comfort.

I won't pretend everything's okay. But I will love him fiercely, even from a distance, because if there's even a chance he finds his way back, I want to be someone he can still come home to.

I used to think love meant sacrifice—giving until I disappeared, holding space until it crushed me, staying silent to keep the peace.

But not anymore. I've found my voice, not just to speak, but to stand. I no longer contort myself to keep others comfortable. I no longer trade my truth for someone else's denial. I say what needs to be said, even when it shakes me, because my peace is no longer up for negotiation.

He is who he is; I am who I am. He doesn't feel things the way I do; he doesn't carry empathy like I do. He doesn't ache with remorse or reflect with the same depth—and that's not mine to change. His journey is his to walk—his lessons, his consequences—they are his alone.

And mine? Mine is to let go of control, to love without rescuing, to protect my peace and honour my growth. I've built myself from the ruins, from the silence, from the dark.

That strength? I earnt it. He may never understand what it took for me to survive, and maybe that's the point. I didn't fight my way through hell so he could repeat it. But if he does, it won't be because I didn't try.

And if he ever turns toward me again, I'll still be here. Not rescuing, not begging, but rooted in truth, in love, in a voice that no longer disappears.

Reflection: - lived experience of the Empty Nest

For decades, my identity was intertwined with being a mum. Every day, someone needed me—someone to feed, comfort, guide, and laugh with. That role brought immense love and satisfaction. I was constantly present, immersed in the joy, chaos, and purpose of motherhood.

As my children grew from infants to toddlers, their needs shifted. They became energetic, demanding, curious little people, and I was there to guide them, chase them, laugh with them, and sometimes tire alongside them. Preschool brought new laughter, imagination, and entertainment, while primary school became a mix of endless school trips, sports, assemblies, and the pride of watching them shine.

Then came secondary school—the dreaded teenage years— where suddenly I wasn't "cool" anymore. Friends took priority, and my hugs were fewer. But through it all, my love remained unwavering. They still came to me for advice, support, and assistance when needed. I learnt that love doesn't always need constant presence; it persists even when they pull away.

Then, almost imperceptibly, they became adults. One blink, and a whole chapter of my life had passed. That huge part of my identity, woven into the fabric of parenting, suddenly felt absent. Free time appeared, silence settled, and I realized I could miss them like crazy.

Worries surfaced—poor choices, risks, dangers—and I struggled with letting go. I wanted to protect them forever, yet I had to face the truth: I never could guarantee safety, no matter how vigilant I was.

Empty nesting is a paradox of freedom and loss. There is joy in the quiet and the time for self, but there is also a profound sense of change and absence. The home feels different, routines shift, and the sense of purpose I relied on for decades must be reimagined.

Grief for the daily presence of my children is normal. Feelings of sadness, nostalgia, and even loneliness are valid. Some days are easier than others. Some days, subtle reminders trigger the longing for earlier times.

Yet, in this new chapter, there is also empowerment, hope, and opportunity. Empty nesting offers space to reconnect with yourself, explore passions that were paused, and nurture relationships beyond parenting.

It is a time to redefine purpose, focus on growth, and celebrate the independent adults you have helped raise. The love between parent and child doesn't vanish—it transforms.

You can continue to support them, cheer for them, and stay connected—but in a new, adult-to-adult way. Learning to step back while staying present is one of the greatest acts of love. You are not losing your children; you are witnessing their growth and resilience. This shift, though challenging, is also a celebration of the life, guidance, and values you instilled.

Hope, Resilience, and Empowerment

Empty nesting is an opportunity for self-discovery. Your life doesn't end when your children leave home—it begins anew.

Pursue hobbies, friendships, and experiences that excite and inspire you. Embrace the freedom to make choices solely for yourself, and remember that the bond with your children is evolving, not ending.

Feelings of loss are natural, but they can coexist with joy, curiosity, and growth. Each phase is temporary, and the relationship with your children deepens in ways that didn't exist before.

Trust in yourself, trust in them, and trust that life has new purposes and rewards waiting.

Supporting Someone Experiencing Empty Nesting – Do's & Don'ts

☑ **DO:**

- Listen without judgment. Let them express nostalgia, sadness, or worry without rushing to reassure.

- Validate their feelings: "It makes sense to miss them" or "It's normal to feel this way."

- Encourage exploration of new hobbies, social groups, or goals.

- Remind them that it's okay to focus on themselves and their own growth.

- Offer companionship and gentle distractions but let them navigate their emotions at their own pace.

- Share stories or examples of others who have found joy in this new chapter.

✖ **DON'T:**

- Don't minimize their feelings. Avoid statements like "They're fine, so you should be too."

- Don't pressure them to "move on" or fill their time immediately.

- Don't dismiss nostalgia or longing, they are natural and important parts of processing change.

- Don't compare their experience to others; everyone adjusts differently.

- Don't imply failure in parenting or that the children leaving means they didn't do a good job.

Key Message:

The empty nest is not an end; it is a transformation. Grief for what was can coexist with excitement for what is possible. Love remains, relationships evolve, and your purpose can be reclaimed and redefined. There is freedom, joy, and empowerment in stepping into this next phase of life fully and authentically.

Chapter 21: When Boundaries Blurred and a crisis broke us

Poem: The Voice That Stayed

I came in silent,

hollowed out by history,

a girl too tired to speak.

You listened

without demand,

and made room for the noise

that had buried itself in my bones.

You taught me to stay.

To breathe.

To feel.

To hope.

And when I asked too much,

you stepped back

not out of hate,

but because you, too,

were human.

Now, I speak alone,

but with your echo still inside me.

You were never mine to keep,

but I will always carry

what you gave:

Hope.

Truth.

Voice.

And the strength

to finally

walk on.

"Some lines are crossed not in harm, but in hope, and when they snap back, they leave no villain, only pain."

I didn't know what to expect that first day of therapy. I wasn't crying. I couldn't cry. I sat stiff on the edge of the chair, afraid to lean back, afraid of being seen. My body was there, but the rest of me—the soul, the spark, the person—was locked somewhere in a freeze I couldn't thaw. I was surviving, nothing more. A hollowed-out version of a girl who had lived through too much and still didn't know how to ask for help.

But she saw me, not as a file, not as a risk assessment or a case note. She greeted me with a bright voice and soft eyes that didn't just fill the space—they held it, held me. Harper didn't just welcome me in; she made me feel like I belonged. Like I was worth knowing. Like I wasn't too broken to begin again.

She used a whiteboard like it was a magic mirror. She translated my metaphors, my silence, my dissociation into language. She mapped out my inner world when I couldn't bear to speak it aloud. Every scribble, every drawn shape, every word became a path out of the trauma I'd been trapped inside for so long. I started breathing again, first in jagged gasps, then in something steady, something real.

Harper wasn't just a therapist. She became so much more: a mentor, a guide, a safe place. Over two years, she sat with me in darkness—through suicidality, panic attacks, grief, and the silent ache of childhood abuse I had never dared name aloud. She didn't flinch. She didn't scold. She didn't shut me down.

She was there, not just as a professional, but as a human.

When I lost my TAFE placement, she stepped up, helping me stay connected to my dream of becoming a peer support worker. She didn't just support me clinically; she believed in me. She created opportunities. She saw something in me I had never dared see in myself.

She reminded me I had value, and I trusted her like I had never trusted anyone before.

Somewhere along the way, the lines between us blurred. It was never intentional. It happened slowly, quietly, like a tide coming in unnoticed until your feet are no longer on dry sand. She replied outside of hours. She offered comfort in ways that extended beyond her role. She let me stay when I had nowhere else safe to go. She became the godparent to my children. I asked her to be the executor of my will.

These were not normal things. They weren't part of a standard therapeutic relationship. But they became our normal—in the name of safety, in the name of care, in the name of connection.

And then came the rupture.

There were early crises—suicide attempts, panic attacks, a phone call made mid-drive when I was spiraling and afraid I wouldn't make it. She stayed on the phone. She spoke to the ambulance with calm authority. She kept me grounded. Another time, I attempted during a phone session from a cemetery. She stayed, held space, breathed with me.

But those moments taught me something I had never been given—they taught me safety, nonjudgment, and support. Each time something happened, I could openly reflect with her and share my gratitude for advocating, for showing up, being persistent, transparent, kind, and empathetic—never someone who scolded or was harsh.

I found acceptance of who I was and felt she accepted me for all my flaws, and she was admiring of all I could achieve. The personal growth, the person who was starting to succeed, the person who could speak safely and reach out to someone instead of using harm and silence to get through the rougher days.

I became more dependent; she became more of a lifeline. I reached deeper into the safety she had offered; she leant further into the space I craved. When I sent a message—an impulsive plea for help laced with pain and poor wording—something snapped.

"Make shit disappear so you don't end up in a coroner's court."

I never meant it as a threat. It was desperation to protect her, not manipulation. But it scared her. She called instead of texting. I couldn't speak. I panicked. I hung up. She sent a welfare check.

And after that… everything changed.

The warmth faded. Her language shifted. Her presence became guarded, distant. A version of her I didn't recognize emerged—clinical, sharp, detached. Not cruel, but cold, like she'd been advised to protect herself. Like she'd been warned, you've gone too far.

She told me a version of events unfolding at that same time, but the timing lined up too neatly. I knew the truth beneath the surface. She had taken my case to supervision. She had seen me as a risk. She was out of her depth. She had realized how far the boundaries had stretched, and the only way to protect herself, and maybe me, was to retreat completely.

Her silence came gently, but it came completely. No more replies. No final conversation. No goodbye. Just distance. Just absence. Just silence. I was gutted.

I had trusted her like no one else. She made me feel safe, and now she was gone. She had become one of them—a person who promised and gave me safety but withdrew it the moment I became too much. I was devastated, abandoned, confused. I didn't know how to make sense of it. She had once told me to always reach out, always speak my truth—and then she disappeared when I needed her most.

And yet… I couldn't hate her. Even through the pain, I still admired her. I still longed for one more conversation, one more explanation, one more moment of clarity. I held out hope, sent an olive branch, a message of honesty, a plea for understanding. But it was met with more silence, and so, I grieved her like a death.

Not the death of a therapist, but the death of a connection. Of a friendship. Of a guide. Of someone I trusted not just with my pain, but with my children, with my future, with every secret I ever carried.

Worse, I was cast once again in the role of the perpetrator—labeled the one who crossed the line. The unstable one. The risk. The liability. The mentally unwell client who asked for too much. In protecting herself, she became silent, and in staying silent, I was left holding all the shame.

But the truth is it wasn't just me. We both went too far. We both blurred the lines. We both acted from care and hope, not harm. We both created something beautiful that couldn't survive within the confines of therapy, and I believe it hurt her, too.

I believe she cared deeply. That she enjoyed watching me grow. That she believed in what we had but didn't know how to bring it back once the boundaries were broken. She did what she had to do to protect her career, her family, her mental health.

I don't fault her for that, but I still hurt. I'm still alone, and I still think of her.

Every time I speak from my truth, I remember that she helped me find it. Every time I support someone else, I remember that she once supported me. She believed in the peer I could become. She saw leadership in me before I did. She planted seeds that still grow, even now.

I walk alone now, but I walk because of her. I can't and I won't allow myself to throw away all our hard work. Though I'll never get the closure I crave, I will always carry the parts of her that live in me—her compassion, her insight, her empathy, her belief in my worth, her human heart that tried so hard to help me heal.

She was never mine to keep, but she will always be someone I carry. The silence didn't end with her last message—it echoes.

It follows me with the thought of entering into new rooms with new therapists, where I will sit stiff again, just like I did the first time with her—except this time, there's no soft voice to coax me in. There's just the memory of what was lost and the fear that if I ever open up like that again, I'll be punished for needing too much.

She taught me trust and safety, then, through no cruel intent but through a rupture neither of us could undo, she showed me what it feels like to lose that trust and safety without a fight. That loss is still bleeding inside me.

I don't hate her. I can't. But I'm still so hurt—hurt that she didn't reply to my olive branch, hurt that I wasn't worth one more conversation, hurt that her voice, once my anchor, became the very absence that tore me adrift.

I question everything now, not just about her but about myself. Was I too much? Was I dangerous? Was I foolish to think what we had was sacred?

I tell myself we both blurred the lines, that it wasn't just me, but the world doesn't see it that way. The world sees the client with mental illness as the unstable one, the one to blame.

I stay silent, not just to protect her reputation, but to avoid further humiliation. Because the moment I speak, I risk being labeled again: manipulative, needy, damaged.

I am grieving, not just her, but the version of myself I was becoming with her guidance. The hope I had, the voice she helped me find, now stuck again behind walls of shame and mistrust. I keep trying to use it—to speak, to connect—but it feels muffled. Like the sound is there, but the world can't hear me.

I miss her. I miss the woman who made me feel safe, who saw me as a whole person, not just a trauma file. Who dreamt with me about the life I could build. Who called herself the

273

godparent to my children. Who gave me her time, her mind, her belief.

I'm confused because the same hands that lifted me up... let go. I don't know if it was fear, or ethics, or supervision that told her she had to.

I just know I was left holding all the grief without any goodbye.

I don't blame her, but I'm still bleeding, and it's hard to move forward when the person who helped you stand is the one you now can't speak to. Can't thank, can't reconcile with, can't even ask: Was I ever really safe? Or did I break the one place I thought I belonged?

That's the cruelty of grief without closure.

I walk forward now because she taught me to. But I do it with a limp, with a voice that still shakes, with a heart that still searches the crowd, hoping to see her face just once—to say thank you, or why, or please don't forget me.

Because I haven't forgotten her, and I never will.

Chapter 22: Searching for Myself in the Mess

Poem: Becoming

I am not broken,

just bending in the storm,

twisting in the winds of pain,

yet here I stand

rooted in the messy soil of survival.

I am not lost,

just wandering through shadows,

searching for my light,

finding strength

in every shattered piece.

I am becoming

a quiet fire burning slow,

a whispered hope rising strong,

a story still unfolding,

raw, real, and true.

And in this becoming,

I find my voice

loud, unashamed,

alive in the mess

that is me.

"I fought for support not just to survive the wreckage inside me, but to stop destroying myself, to uncover the fragments of who I was, and to stitch them into a self I could finally believe in, strong, worthy, and my own."

I have lost every support, every hand I used to lean on, alone again, exhausted and scared. Not the loud kind of fear that screams, but the silent, suffocating kind that fills every inch until breathing feels like drowning.

Life's weight crushes me: grief, noise, exhaustion, and the crushing pressure of trying to be okay when I am anything but. The dark thoughts come crawling back, old familiar monsters I know too well. They whisper, pulling me toward the edge, toward the places I swore I'd never return. I know where they lead, but this time, I refuse. This time, I won't lose myself again.

The urges to self-harm roar inside me like a firestorm. I crave something sharp, something real, a release from invisible pain that claws at my insides. Physical pain is twisted comfort; it's a reset I know how to handle. But I don't act, I can't, not this time, because now I work in suicide prevention. I'm the one telling others, "There's always another way." Now I must live that truth myself.

I shout at those voices, beg for silence, for peace, even if just for one moment. But they circle, relentless and fierce, clawing at the edges of my mind.

At home, chaos swirls. Mark spirals—disrespectful, entitled, breaking rules like they don't exist. Bikes roar through the streets at all hours, illegal driving, in and out of the house like I'm invisible. The noise, the fear, the ache of being dismissed by my own son—it crushes me.

I reach a breaking point; I ban him from the house for 48 hours. No compromises; lies must stop, respect must start. I do it to protect my fragile mind and because I don't want to bury my child.

Then I reach out, I make myself accountable, I name my feelings, my fears, the hopelessness I feel. I call ROSES for support, followed by Community Mental Health. I ask for a referral to STRIDE & THRIVE—no more falling into the dark rabbit hole. Instead, I buckle up tight to fight the rough ride.

This could be my way out. If I go to STRIDE & THRIVE, I will have safety, accountability, a place to breathe, to heal, to find me again.

When I book the recovery camp, my brain screams, "Don't go! Don't let them see you broken." But I am proud—proud I'm fighting back, proud I'm doing the opposite of what I used to. The voices want to pull me under; they tell me I'm worthless, undeserving, but I fight back.

Recovery camp week arrives. Anxiety crashes over me like a tidal wave. I'm physically sick; my ears ache. I finally see a doctor when the pain is too bad to manage. Diagnosed with a double middle ear infection, handed antibiotics. In the end, the pain, the temperature, and the anxiety riddled my exhausted body, so I made the ultimate decision: I don't go to recovery camp.

The disappointment suffocates me; I tell myself I can't do people anymore. Isolation feels safer, but I know, deep inside, those are lies—depression's claws trying to drag me back down.

I don't give up; I push for STRIDE & THRIVE. I need somewhere familiar, somewhere healing is allowed.

Then, unexpectedly, I am called for a peer support job, chased using an old résumé for a prior position I applied for. Not daring to hope—if I don't try hard, the rejection won't hurt so much. If I didn't believe it would happen and things were looking up, then the crash wouldn't be so hard if the result isn't the future I had always dreamt of.

A second call comes—not a rejection, but a callback. They want my story, more in-depth questioning into my journey toward recovery. I tell them the truth—I'm in the middle of a storm. I expect dismissal, but instead, they shortlist me for an in-person interview.

An opening, a step further than I had been in employment in the last three years. Shock, fear, pride swirl inside me. I feel like a fraud, but I take it, cling to that flicker of hope—maybe I'm enough.

STRIDE & THRIVE intake hits me hard, old files pulled up, past twisted into shameful stories. I feel punched in the gut—not seen as a person but as a problem. No warmth, no kindness, only judgment. I'm exposed and raw, yet communicating transparently with every ounce of strength I have left.

There was no Zoom link sent for the meeting. I feel forgotten, erased, victim-blamed for not being online. No duty of care or respect, no checking in with me—just short, abrupt conversation. I nearly walk away.

I remember why I asked for help—because I want to find myself again. Because I am not what happened to me. Because I am worthy of recovery. Because I believe in the work I do. Because I want to live.

So, I show up—anxious, sweaty, stomach twisting, shaking with fright. I glue my feet to the floor and drown out the noisy thoughts once again yelling, "Give up the fight, run away, do what you know works, hit your reset." But I show up. I step into the unknown and let a sliver of light in.

In those rooms, I keep telling myself: don't undo your progress, don't let the darkness win. I fight, I claw, bruised and scarred, but I am here. Every step aches because healing is supposed to hurt—it must be real.

I can't let my past define me; my trauma must have been for something. It must shape me to help others from truth, not theory; from empathy, not ego; from survival, strength, and stubborn hope.

This is only the beginning. I am here. I am becoming.

It has been only 24 hours since I entered STRIDE & THRIVE, but the outside world pulls hard.

My phone rings—Jennifer is crying, friendship drama, more weight on my shoulders. I want to be her anchor, her calm. But this is my time—the strong, selfish feelings and emotions wash over me in waves. Torn between staying for time I carved out to put myself back together or running home to hold and fix the one who means the most to me.

Guilt rises—Jennifer's with Karen, stressed, holding too much already. Now a friend treats Jennifer badly. The old urge to fix it, rush home, be the safe place, pulls fiercely.

Rational voice screams—even when I'm home, Jennifer hides; she's with the ones she trusts, and I'm not one of them right now. So, I stop. I breathe. I remind myself: she is safe, she is loved. If I don't help myself now, I can't keep helping her through life. I support her from a distance, let her know she's loved and I care. This helps in protecting us both.

Then Mark—his mates are at the house despite my rules. He knows if I'm home, they wouldn't be there. Without me, respect disappears, rules don't matter. Noise at 3 a.m., TV blasting, music shaking the walls, waking Jennifer.

I send a calm but firm message, a reminder: respect matters, always. I don't spiral; I breathe; I set boundaries; I come back to me.

I can't pour into others if I'm empty. STRIDE & THRIVE is about filling myself up piece by piece—rest, belief, clarity, rebuilding strength buried beneath years of exhaustion.

The job interview looms; I have been granted leave to attend. It feels like a sign—someone sees potential in me. I prepare not just for the interview but for the chance to be seen for my worth—a chance for growth, a return to a purpose and normality of employment I once loved the most.

Doubt whispers, "You're not enough," but I answer back: "I'm still here; that matters—it means something." I stay, show up to groups, breathe through guilt and noise. I choose me. I'm not escaping life; I'm rebuilding it, minute by minute—that's my goal: to stay alive.

The interview day arrives; I wear a little makeup, not to hide but to honor myself. I'm neat, casual, authentic—no masks. Three people sit across from me; their questions could shake me once, but now I listen deeply. I answer honestly, no rehearsed lines, no sugarcoating, just the raw truth from my scars.

I hold my head high; I speak with calm, clarity, and quiet confidence. If I don't get the job, it's okay because I did the impossible. I showed up, took space, spoke my truth, and left proud—that's my win.

I don't let self-doubt silence me. I show up because of my past, not despite it. Now I wait—a call, an email, a sign. I double-check who the referees I will give if they do contact me again. ROSES says yes immediately—warm, supportive—a lift to my spirit.

Then Harper—I hesitate to ask her, so much pain between us. Fear of rejection, but she says yes; relief floods me. Maybe respect still lives beneath the cracks.

I check emails daily—hope without desperation, belief that maybe I'm enough.

Back at STRIDE & THRIVE, only two of us remain. The quiet feels different—peaceful but lonely.

The end nears; I write letters to those who touched me deeply—Elisabeth, Skyla, Edward, Brooke, Indi the clinician.

Letter to Elisabeth

Elisabeth's support was constant, her warmth a beacon in my darkest times. Her laughter lightened heavy days, and her unwavering belief in me planted seeds of hope. I thanked her for seeing me beyond the chaos, for never giving up, for pushing me to be kinder to myself.

When she read my letter, tears welled up in her eyes. She struggled with the gratitude, unsure how to respond but visibly moved. Her gentle hug said more than words.

Letter to Skyla

Skyla was the steady presence I clung to when the storm raged. I thanked her for listening without judgment, for offering gentle strength when I felt weak, for reminding me I was not alone.

Her eyes shimmered with emotion; she told me quietly that my words gave her hope—hope that healing is possible.

Letter to Edward

Edward's humour was a salve to my soul. Even when I felt raw and fragile, he could make me laugh until my cheeks ached. I told him how his lightness saved me, how his encouragement fuelled my fight.

Edward read my letter aloud, his voice cracking. Tears slipped freely down his face. "You've got more strength than you know," he said softly.

Letter to Indi, the clinician

Indi was a guardian of my story. I thanked her for creating a safe space to share the parts I hid even from myself, for reading my memoir with care and respect, for helping me find words when I had none.

Indi paused, overwhelmed. Her tears betrayed her struggle with the vulnerability of my truth. "Thank you for trusting me," she whispered.

Letter to Brooke

Brooke—bubbly, warm, a constant energizer. She taught me to make a key ring at my first stay, which sparked my love for beading and crafts. She always listened, never judged. Brooke kept it real, inspired me, made the journey lighter.

When Brooke read her letter, she smiled through tears. "You've come so far," she said, her voice thick with pride. "You inspire me too."

Giving these letters was as much healing for me as for them. The staff were deeply touched; some struggled with the positive feedback, unsure how to receive it but grateful beyond words. I saw in their eyes that my gratitude mattered as much as their support.

I walked out of STRIDE & THRIVE with pride and satisfaction. I had done something proactive; I had stuck it out, and I had been true to myself.

Staff told me I had a future in peer work, that I had potential. Their belief was a balm to my soul.

Though the job never came through, I won't give up. Helping others heals me. It's the therapy I need most.

The call came like a stone dropped into my chest. I listened as they told me I hadn't been successful. When they offered feedback, I clung to it, desperate for something to hold on to. At first, their words wrapped around me like sunlight breaking through clouds—how well I had interviewed, how clearly my passion shone, how I was diverse, client-centered, respectful of clients' rights, mindful of my own bias.

They told me I carried the strength of lived experience, that they saw the value I could bring as a peer worker. My heart swelled, beating with hope. Then came the pause, followed by the word that cut the air between us—but everything inside me dropped.

They explained that, unlike the other applicants, I didn't have paid experience. The encouragement at the end of the call felt hollow, like a door closing gently but firmly in my face.

When I hung up, the silence in the room pressed down on me. Tears slid down my cheeks until I was shaking with quiet sobs, my chest aching with the weight of what could have been. Yet beneath the grief, something stirred—a stubborn thread of determination that refused to be broken. Wiping my face, I opened my resume, made tweaks, and reached out for new references. If they couldn't see me yet, I would make sure the next time they had no choice.

I'm anxious to return home—Mark, who I must keep on track; Jennifer, who is retreating too much. I fear she carries my DNA, the battles with mental health that have marked me.

But I close this chapter on a high note—I did it. I gave it my best; I stayed true to myself. My best is enough; I won't let the negative voices say otherwise.

Reflection: The Power of Peer Support

In my own journey, I came to see a very clear difference between clinical support and peer support. Clinical spaces often felt focused on risk, legal obligations, and ethics.

They came with a tick-box and "fix-it" approach that sometimes felt controlling or even frightening. The professional hierarchy, while necessary in many ways, created a gap.

It was hard to form a genuine connection when I felt I was being assessed, judged, or managed rather than truly understood.

Peer support was different.

Peer support workers sat beside me, not above me. They met me where I was, without time limits, without judgment, without pressure to fit into a box or a treatment plan.

With peer support, I felt seen, heard, and valued as a person, not just a case file or a set of symptoms.

The difference was profound. Peer supporters offered:

- **Empathy**, a real, lived understanding of pain and survival.

- **Compassion**, being with me in my hardest moments without trying to take over.

- **Connection**, sharing humanity, not hierarchy.

- **Non-judgment**, holding space for every part of me, even the parts I found hard to accept.

- **Autonomy and choice**, reminding me that my voice mattered and that I had the power to decide what healing looked like for me.

When I spoke with peers, I felt a weight lift off me. Saying things out loud, in a safe and supported space, helped me discover what was really overwhelming me. They didn't fix me; they walked beside me, which gave me the courage and clarity to find my own way forward.

Hope, Resilience, and Empowerment

Peer support taught me that healing is not about being "fixed," because I was never broken. It's about being witnessed, respected, and believed. It's about having someone by your side who understands that pain is real but so is hope.

What peers model so powerfully is resilience in action—showing that survival is possible, that growth is possible, and that our voices matter. They help break down shame by normalizing our struggles and highlighting our strengths.

The wisdom I carry from peer support is this:

- Healing happens in connection.

- Hope grows when it is shared.

- We are never as alone as we fear.

- Our stories matter, and when spoken, they can set us free.

If you are struggling, reaching out to a peer may be the first step in finding the courage to heal. Peer support doesn't replace clinical care when it's needed, but it offers something unique—the reminder that you are not broken, you are not a burden, and you are not alone.

Supporting Someone Through Peer Support

☑ **Do:**

- Meet people where they are, not where you think they should be.

- Listen with empathy, not with an agenda.

- Share lived experience only when it's useful to the other person.

- Encourage autonomy and choice, empower, don't direct.

- Sit in silence if that's what's needed, presence speaks volumes.

- Hold hope, even when the person can't hold it themselves.

- Be consistent, reliable, and authentic.

- Validate feelings, even the messy, confusing ones.

✕ **Don't:**

- Don't try to "fix" or rescue.

- Don't judge, shame, or minimise their experience.

- Don't take over or control the direction of their healing.

- Don't create hierarchy, you are walking beside them, not above them.

- Don't rush or pressure them into sharing more than they're ready to.

- Don't compare struggles or make it about your story instead of theirs.

- Don't dismiss small wins, every step matters.

Key Message

Clinical support has its place and can be lifesaving, but peer support brings something equally powerful: connection without hierarchy, empathy without judgment, and hope without conditions.

Together, clinical and peer support can complement one another, but it is often in peer spaces where we finally feel safe enough to speak our truth, free enough to be ourselves, and strong enough to take the next step forward.

Chapter 23: Where the Stigma Ends, Healing Begins

Poem: Where the Stigma Ends, Healing Begins

The headset hums,

and so does my heart

a frantic drum

afraid of failing.

My voice quivers at hello,

but then… silence holds me,

and I learn to trust the caller's lead,

to follow their story

like a trail through dark woods.

I listen,

not with ears alone

but with the ache of my own scars,

with the part of me

that has sat in shadows

and longed for a hand,

any hand,

to reach back.

Their courage stuns me

to dial, to speak,

to shatter the loneliness of a closed room.

And in their words,

I hear my own once-broken whispers,

now softened into strength.

We breathe together.

We sift pain from silence.

I offer not answers

but space,

a mirror of compassion

where their truth can stand unshaken.

And when their voice shifts

from trembling to steady,

from heavy to lighter

something inside me lifts too.

The weight of my past

is not erased,

but reshaped.

What once burnt

now warms.

What once broke me

now blooms.

I hang up each call

with gratitude swelling

not for saving anyone,

but for witnessing,

for being trusted

to cradle another's story

while growing gentler

with my own.

"I didn't need saving from myself, I needed to be witnessed without fear, so that my silence could break, and my story could breathe in the light."

I was searching not just for a way to volunteer, but for a place where my experience, my pain, and my hard-won wisdom could mean something. Somewhere I could give back but also belong and fit in.

That day, scrolling through Indeed, an ad caught my eye: Roses in the Ocean. They were looking for people to do training to make callbacks on their warm line, a suicide prevention service. My heart skipped a beat. I'd never heard of them before, but something about the name, soft and fragile yet defiant, pulled at me.

I clicked through to their website, and it felt like stepping into another world. The homepage was alive with possibilities: workshops, stories, connections, training, calls for volunteers.

Every word seemed to hum with invitation: "Your voice matters here, your story can help someone survive, you belong." My chest tightened with excitement, and my stomach fluttered with nerves. Could this really be real? Could there actually be a place where my scars weren't something to hide but something that gave me purpose?

I devoured every page. I saw the workshops, the training sessions, the online Zoom options, and I felt a spark of hope I hadn't felt in years. The thought of being in a room, even virtually, with strangers who understood, who carried their own battles, made my heart race with anticipation.

Yet anxiety prickled at the edges: What if I wasn't ready? What if I said the wrong thing? What if I couldn't handle hearing the pain of someone else? My fingers hovered over the sign-up button as I wrestled with both fear and longing.

Finally, I clicked, and suddenly a rush of joy flooded me—a quiet, trembling joy that this could be the beginning of something I had been searching for all my life: a place where I could belong, where my voice could matter. Where I could use the hardest parts of myself to bring light into someone else's darkness. Even the uncertainty felt alive, electric, like stepping onto the edge of something big, something I didn't yet fully understand but deeply needed.

I found the Zoom training sessions and signed up, promising myself that I could leave at any time if the anxiety became too much. But deep down, I knew I wouldn't. Something told me that this was where I had been heading all along—a place where the ache of my past could transform into connection, purpose, and finally, relief.

The first workshop I attended was casual, yet quietly intense. Small groups, capped at ten participants with two facilitators, created a sense of closeness I hadn't expected. The room, even though it was a Zoom screen, felt almost tangible, like I could reach through and touch the presence of everyone there.

Knowledge and perspective weren't just coming from the facilitators; they were in the pauses between people's words, in the trembling way someone might share a story, in the sighs, the quiet nods, the almost imperceptible shivers of recognition.

I had experienced suicide through three lenses: my own inner battles, the struggles of people I loved, and the endless attempts that I lost count of. But the lens I had never known, the one that left a mark deep in my chest, was bereavement.

Hearing stories of loss, grief spilling raw and unfiltered from people who had survived it, shook something loose inside me. It wasn't just knowledge; it was something I could feel in my bones. The ache of loss, the quiet trembling, the suffocating emptiness—I understood it in a way I hadn't before.

There was no hierarchy, no power, no dominance, just an equal playing field—a gentle space where connection could grow. The atmosphere was soft, supportive but intense.

Workshop Two went deeper. This was where we began to explore how to take our stories, our lived experiences, and share them in ways that could support someone else. I struggled here, not because I didn't belong, but because the kindness of everyone overwhelmed me.

My heart thumped painfully against my ribs. For the first time, I was truly seen, heard, and validated—not silenced, corrected, or judged. The weight of finally being accepted for exactly who I was almost unbearable.

Being able to speak about suicide and have it received with acceptance hit me like a wave. My vision blurred with tears, my chest tightened—a mixture of joy and panic. I couldn't breathe properly.

I had to leave the Zoom. I left the room, but not the warmth of the space. Gentle texts arrived almost immediately, checking in on me. No pressure, no control, no demands—just concern, care, and an invitation, freedom to respond in my own time.

I wanted to talk, but my voice was stuck, muted by the fear of past experiences with services—the involuntary interventions, the policing of my life, the control taken from me over and over.

I curled into a ball in my room, trembling, rocking slightly, trying to make sense of the chaos inside my mind. Tears rolled down my face, unbidden, carrying joy, relief, fear, and sadness all at once. My brain felt like a tightly coiled ball of string, impossible to untangle.

More texts, more gentle calls—they didn't demand answers, didn't push me. Slowly, cautiously, I felt a spark of courage flicker. I picked up the phone and dialed back. My chest thudded violently.

What if I had ruined my chance to volunteer on the warm line? What if they saw me as fragile, broken, too much? But on the other end, I was met with empathy, compassion, and reassurance. No punishment, no judgment—I could breathe, truly breathe, for the first time in what felt like years.

As I began to speak, carefully picking at the tangles inside me, the coordinator listened without interruption. When the question about my safety came, my chest seized again. My mind flashed back to police, involuntary orders, power stripped from me, control taken away—panic surged.

But this time, it was met with patience. I was told I didn't have to answer; it didn't matter. I felt safe. A weight I hadn't known I was carrying lifted from my chest, a burden I hadn't dared to name quietly dissolving.

I spoke for a long time, slowly navigating my feelings, untangling the messy knots of my mind with someone there to hold them with care. Every emotion, fear, sadness, shame, relief was welcomed and acknowledged.

When I finally said thank you and goodbye, I felt lighter, calmer, and for the first time in a long while, safe. I had been heard, validated, and reassured. I had spoken my truth and, for once, it had not been used against me.

I had not been judged; I had not been silenced; I had been met with humanity. In that moment, I began to feel the faint stirrings of hope—that healing, belonging, and connection were possible.

I found Roses in the Ocean to be a place where I could safely unmask—a space where I could speak my truth and never be shut down. For the first time in a long while, I was met with acceptance—a word I rarely allow myself to use, yet here it felt fitting. I felt normal in a way I hadn't felt for years, no longer the only person living with suicidality. For once, I belonged and was no longer left feeling alone.

I went on to do more workshops, diving deeper into the training, exploring both the practical skills and the human connection that underpinned everything. Each workshop felt the same in the best way—a space of warmth, safety, and connection.

Knowledge flowed not just from the facilitators but from participants themselves—from their honesty, their courage, their presence. Most workshops ran for two days, but those forty-eight hours often felt like being wrapped in a network of family—invisible hugs, quiet nods of recognition, the soft reassurance of empathy and compassion. I was surrounded by people who truly understood, people who got me without needing explanations or apologies.

There was no judgment, no shame, no mask, no fear of being fully myself. I even began to confidently text if anxiety was going to make me late, knowing I would be met with understanding rather than criticism.

Each workshop ended with a feeling I had never known—lighter, more confident, and with personal insight that felt earnt, not taught. I walked away feeling not damaged but growing, learning to accept that my experiences, even the painful ones, were a part of who I was, not a definition of me.

Slowly, the narrative I had carried for so long began to shift. I was no longer "broken" or "wrong." Those words were replaced with recovery, with acceptance, with the knowledge that life was a roller coaster—a series of turbulent waves I could navigate with support. My mental health challenges weren't the sum of me; they were a part of me, yes, but they didn't define me. They were snippets of experience, behaviours, and patterns—pieces of a much larger, resilient whole.

With the support of Roses in the Ocean, everything became more bearable, more possible, and far easier to live with. I began to feel strength where there had once been shame, clarity where there had once been chaos, and hope where despair had often lingered.

For the first time, I could see that my story—all of it, the pain and the survival, the fear and the triumph—had value. In that, I found not just relief but purpose, connection, and, finally, a place I could truly call home.

When I finished my training for the warm line, I felt both excited and terrified. The idea of making my first call filled me with nerves that buzzed through my body like electricity. I was scared I would get it wrong, scared I would stumble, scared I would fail someone in their moment of need. The weight of that responsibility pressed heavily on my chest.

But as soon as I introduced myself to the caller and let them begin, the nerves slowly shifted. The more I listened, the steadier I felt. I realized I didn't have to have all the answers—there was no right or wrong; the difference really came from holding space for the caller.

I let them guide, and in that, I felt a deep sense of privilege—to be trusted with their words, their silence, their pain. To sit with them, even just through a phone line, was sacred.

Every call left me empowered. At the end of each conversation, I carried with me a sense of connection, a quiet joy in knowing that listening—truly listening—could make such a difference.

Sharing small, powerful, and hopeful parts of my own story when it felt right helped build rapport, but more than that, it reminded the caller that they weren't alone. Sometimes I could hear the shift in their voice—a softening, a release, a spark of hope creeping back in. Those shifts felt like miracles.

I learnt that deep listening, understanding, and validation could have a huge impact. It wasn't about rescuing or fixing; it was about being present with empathy, compassion, and no judgment. Callers already carried strength; they already held the answers within themselves.

All I could do was gently reflect that back to them. The courage it takes for someone to pick up the phone—to speak into the silence—is immense. I always made sure to highlight that courage, that bravery, that strength—because sometimes people forget their own light.

Often what callers needed most was space to vent, to let the mess tumble out, to hear their own voice aloud, to not feel alone. That simple act of expression helped them shift focus, even just a little. Each time, I felt honoured and privileged to be there in that moment, to witness it, to hold it.

I love what I do, and I love how it makes me feel. Being part of the warm line reframes my own pain and trauma. Instead of being a source of shame, it becomes something meaningful, something warm, something that connects me to others. The negative lens I had carried for so long—the belief that my story made me broken—was replaced by a sense of purpose and even joy.

The positive impact was always first for the callers, but it was also profoundly rewarding for me. Each conversation left me not drained but filled—filled with hope, filled with gratitude, filled with the reminder that even out of the darkest places, something beautiful can grow.

Roses in the Ocean holds values and respect that deeply align with me personally. They don't just talk the talk; they walk it. What they stand for isn't about looking good on paper—it's lived and real. Their advocacy and constant fight for change are incredible, and I've never experienced anything like it with any other organization, mental health or otherwise.

The way they genuinely understand and challenge the clinical system to create equality for lived experience truly blows me away. I don't think Roses in the Ocean fully realizes the positive impact they have. For me, they've been a lifeline, helping me get through the past few challenging months without an attempt—that, in itself, is proof of the difference they make.

I was introduced to more peer-led supports, services called Discharged and Alt2Su. When I mentioned them to my therapist, she frowned and admitted she didn't like the sound of them. I could see the concern in her eyes—the kind that came from a professional's perspective, shaped by fear and training. What she couldn't see was how much hope these spaces held for me.

Discharged was a peer-led community—a space built by people who had stood in the darkest corners of despair and decided to build lanterns there for others.

Alt2Su was another lifeline, a network where people came together not to push each other into death but to sit with the raw ache of wanting to escape it. These were not reckless spaces, as some professionals feared. They were sacred ones—honest, unpolished, real.

When the storm inside me raged and I felt that familiar pull into the abyss, I would log on—sometimes trembling, sometimes numb—and there, I wasn't met with judgment, clinical notes, or alarmed faces that wanted to "fix" me.

Instead, I was met with open arms, words typed out across screens that felt warmer than most rooms I'd sat in: "I hear you." "You're not alone." "It's okay to feel like this." I could breathe in those spaces.

No one demanded I silence my pain; no one tightened their grip to control me. I was never told I was dangerous or broken. Instead, they offered me reassurance, validation, and space to speak freely or to just sit silently, knowing I was still being held. The dignity in that was something I didn't even know I was starving for until I found it.

Some days I went there to pour my own pain out. Other days, I stayed to hold space for someone else—to offer the same presence that had saved me. It was a cycle of giving and receiving—no hierarchy, no judgment, just humanity.

Professionals often paint groups like these as dens of danger, as if we're all gathered around whispering encouragement to die. But that's not the truth. The truth is that most of us didn't want to die—we just wanted the pain to stop.

We wanted to escape, release, not vanish. These groups weren't death clubs—they were survival groups, in the rawest, truest sense of the word. They were no different than NA or AA or GA, except that we dared to say the word suicide out loud. Because of that, we were branded as shameful, dangerous, evil.

But in those rooms, I felt none of that. I felt freedom, autonomy, dignity, respect—a sense of being safe enough to take off the mask I wore everywhere else. There was no pressure to perform, no demands to speak, no agenda to "fix" me. Just gentle curiosity, kindness, and the safety to grow at my own pace.

Here's the truth that shakes me even now: since finding these services, I haven't once made an attempt on my life—not once. That's an incredible difference, moving from every 3–6 weeks with an occasional six-month streak. Yes, I've had dark days, but I've fought instead of giving in.

The thoughts still come—of course, the dark days don't vanish overnight—but I know now how to ride them out. I can reach for help without guilt, without shame. I can say, "I'm struggling," and not fear being locked away or silenced.

These three services didn't just help me—they saved me. They gave me the chance to grow roots in a place I never thought anything could survive.

They taught me that I wasn't evil, I wasn't weak, and I wasn't alone.

I am no longer backed into a corner—no longer swallowing shame for feelings I can't always control. I'm always on the lookout; I am still fighting but no longer alone. Yes, I still fall, but now, when I do, I reach out to those I know are safe. They sit with me in the dark until I can see the light again.

I remain cautious with professionals because so many still treat suicide as something to fear, something to silence, something to control. That fear builds walls between us. But with my safe people—those who truly see me—I know I don't have to hide.

I won't be controlled, I won't be silenced, I won't mask the most human parts of me just to make others comfortable. Instead, I will keep speaking, I will keep feeling, I will keep reaching, and I will keep surviving.

Epilogue

When I first began writing this memoir, it wasn't for anyone else's eyes. I started simply as a way to cope, to journal, to vent, to put words to a reality I had carried in silence for far too long.

Writing became a tool, a lifeline. It allowed me to clear my headspace, to put my truth into words, and to begin the slow, difficult work of acceptance. On the page, I could make sense of things that had always felt senseless. Writing gave me perspective, clarity, and, at times, healing.

As I kept writing, I discovered something unexpected: my words could travel beyond me. When I struggled to explain myself, or when I couldn't bear to re-speak my trauma, I began sharing the chapters with people who needed to understand.

Each time I did, something shifted. The feedback reminded me that truth has power. The act of rereading my own words gave me perspective; it showed me how far I had come, and it sparked the thought that maybe my story could do the same for others.

This journey has been long. For most of my life, my childhood memories were buried, pushed down under layers of survival mode. I didn't realize it then how much of myself I was holding back just to keep going.

From 2022 through 2025, I faced some of my darkest struggles yet. Suicidality hovered closely, fuelled by repeated traumatic events. For a long time, I existed in a cycle of barely living. But slowly, piece by piece, the shift came.

I began to choose life; I began to move from surviving to truly living. With that shift, my light, though fragile, began to shine again.

I am not free from pain. I live with complex PTSD, anxiety, depression, suicidality, and most likely ADHD. These parts of me don't vanish, but I've learnt they also don't define me.

I have dark days still, but now I have tools, safe people, and the strength to reach out without shame when I need help. I accept these things as part of me, but not the whole of me.

I am not broken! I am not damaged! I am a survivor!

I watch out for those strong, sudden dives into the depths, but I also know I have anchors now. Tools, wisdom, connection. These are the things that have carried me to this point, and they are what I want to share.

If you are reading this, I hope you gained from my story not only education and understanding but also connection, hope, and maybe even a little strength to keep going.

I know I am one of the lucky ones. I survived suicide. I survived myself. Because of that, I now have the privilege to share my wisdom with others, to turn my pain into something meaningful.

So here is what I leave you with: keep moving forward, reach out, connect, keep dreaming. When life has meaning, purpose, connection, and hope, there is always strength to carry on.

Dream big, aim high, share your lived experience, because it is not a burden, it is a superpower. When you flip your narrative, you flip the lens through which you see the world. When that shift happens, you open your eyes to so much more than survival. You open your eyes to life, a new belief system, and begin truly living.

Closing poem

The Journey Back to Life

I walked a road of shattered glass,

bare feet bleeding from the past.

Silent screams, a heart held tight,

living shadows in endless night.

CPTSD carved its scars,

etched in memory, written in stars.

I thought survival was all there'd be,

but even pain can set us free.

Through connection, I found a hand,

someone who chose to understand.

In mirrors of hope, my truth was seen,

no longer lost, I could begin.

Identity returned in fragments, slow,

like seedlings pushing through the snow.

Meaning whispered, soft and clear:

"You are still here. You are still here."

Empowerment rose where shame once lay,

self-reflection lit the way.

Resilience grew from roots below,

therapy teaching what hearts can know.

As I walk this journey wide,

with joy and laughter at my side.

With friends, with love, with truth, with fun,

the healing path is never done.

For every inner child must play,

to dance the dark and sing the day.

A life reclaimed, a spirit whole,

connection stitching back the soul.

Australian helpful resources and contacts
Peer supports services

Roses in the Ocean – National lived-experience of suicide organisation offering peer support via the Peer CARE Companion Warmline and also community workshops and resources.

Contact: Warmline callback service: 1800 777 337 (leave message, callback within 48 hrs)

Online -www.rosesintheocean.com.au

Discharged – Peer-led support groups for those with suicidal thoughts or experiences, focusing on open dialogue without clinical intervention.

online- www.discharged.asn.au

Alternatives to Suicide (Alt2Su) – Peer-led, non-clinical support groups (online and in-person) for people with suicidal thoughts.

Online- www.alt2su-nsw.net

Crisis support contacts

1800RESPECT –Free 24/7 National confidential counselling and support service for people affected by domestic, family, or sexual violence.

Contact: Phone: 1800 737 732   Text: 0458 737 732

Online chat & video call www.1800respect.org.au

Kids Helpline – Free, 24/7 counselling via phone, online chat, and email for ages 5–25. Covers topics like sexual abuse, mental health, and more.

Contact: Phone: 1800 551 800   Email: counsellor@kidshelpline.com.au (8 am–10 pm)

Online www.kidshelpline.com.au

Lifeline – Free 24/7 crisis support and suicide prevention via phone, text, or online chat.

Contact: 13 11 14   text 0477 13 11 14

Online www.lifeline.org.au

Beyond Blue – Free 24/7 Offers information and counselling services for depression, anxiety, suicide prevention, and support services.

Contact: 1300 22 4636

Online www.beyondblue.org.au

Suicide Call Back Service – Free 24/7 phone and online counselling for people affected by suicide.

Contact: 1300 659 467

Online www.suicidepreventionaust.org

MensLine Australia - free 24/7 telephone and online counselling for men with concerns about mental health, anger, family violence, relationship and stress.

Contact: 1300 78 99 78

Online www.mensline.org.au

13YARN – Culturally safe crisis supports for Aboriginal and Torres Strait Islander people.

Contact: 13 92 76

Online www.13yarn.org.au

QLife – LGBTIQ+ peer support and referral service.

Contact: 1800 184 527 (3 pm–midnight)

Online www.qlife.org.au

Education, self-help supports

Blue knot- Blue Knot is a national centre of excellence for complex trauma, providing information, support, resources and training for survivors, supporters and professionals. **Contact:** 1300 657 380 Mon – Sun 9am – 5pm email helpline@blueknot.org.au

Online www.blueknot.org.au

Sane- Choose from a range of FREE complex mental health supports, including recovery programs with counselling, peer support and/or groups, 24/7 community forums, events, and information and resources.

Online www.sane.org

Preplanned preferences of wishes

Voluntary Disclosure of Personal Information – Victoria Police

This is a process where you can choose to share important personal information with Victoria Police about how you'd like to be approached or supported if they need to interact with you. It could include things like communication preferences, disability support needs, or mental health considerations. The information is securely stored on a national database so police across Australia can access it if needed.

Website:

www.police.vic.gov.au/voluntary-disclosure-personal-information

Advance Care Directive / Advance Care Planning Forms

These forms allow you to record your healthcare preferences in advance, so your wishes are respected if you become too unwell to make or communicate decisions yourself. They can include choices about medical treatments, hospital care, and who you'd like to act as your decision-maker (substitute decision-maker). Having this in place ensures your voice is heard even if you are in crisis or admitted involuntarily.

Website:

www.health.vic.gov.au/patient-care/advance-care-planning-forms

www.ingramcontent.com/pod-product-compliance
Lightning Source LLC
Chambersburg PA
CBHW071711120626
46550CB00001B/187